I Didn't Realise I was Old

Thoughts on reaching 60 years of age

RS Bridger

Contents

Introduction

I didn't realise I was old until I went for haircut a while back and the hairdresser asked me if I wanted my eyebrows trimmed. The next thing I knew she was snipping away at the hair in my ears.

When I got home, nobody even noticed I'd had a haircut (not enough hair).

Twenty-one days ago, before my 60th birthday, I decided to keep a diary. Sixty year olds get free prescriptions at the Chemists in England, a Senior Citizen's Railcard, discounted membership fees at the tennis club and special deals at the fish and chip shop.

So, there's a lot to look forward to.

All these goodies and with everyone being nice to you for a change, it really brings it home. When I was a young man, I thought of 60 year olds as old people. Now, I'm not so sure. They say that old age brings forgetfulness, but how would I know? I can't remember having been forgetful recently.

Approaching this milestone in life (which is about as exciting as being late for work on a Tuesday morning) I decided to keep a daily diary, just in case there was anything worth remembering in the run-up to senility. Maybe it's worth recording one's thoughts and experiences as one's sixtieth birthday bears down, like time pressing on a full bladder.

Day 21: A Romantic Dinner for Two.

I decided to take my wife out for a romantic dinner at our local Thai restaurant. We went fairly early in the evening because we find late nights challenging and would rather be asleep in bed. The restaurant was very welcoming with candlelit tables and subdued South East Asian decoration. The waiter showed us to our table and we sat down. He handed us the wine list and the menu and walked away. After chatting for while we looked at the menu.

We couldn't read a word of it.

Unfortunately, we had both forgotten to bring our reading glasses and we coped by ordering a set meal for two and a pint and a half of house lager.

Old age can catch up with you when you are least expecting it, I've found. I tried to make light of it.

'There's something wrong with the electricity these days' I said. They don't make it like they used to. When I was young and you turned the lights on everything was lit brightly and things shone with vivid colours. Nowadays, we're stuck with this green electricity made out of wind and not proper electricity made out of coal or uranium, like we used to have years ago.' My wife smiled back patiently and politely in the way that people do when they don't share one's sense of humour.

Fortunately, new technology has come to our rescue. At dinner in a Tapas Bar, a few weeks later, we found ourselves in a similar situation and my clever wife used the torch app on her smart phone to illuminate the menu and we were able to get by. When it came to the wine list, she photographed it and we zoomed in on the image of the list so we could read it. It didn't make a great deal of difference on this occasion, because we would have ordered the Rioja anyway, although it probably saved us a couple of quid. Even old people can learn new skills when they have to.

Day 20: I Saw Myself on TV in a History Programme

I was sitting in the lounge the other day watching a television documentary about Britain in the 1970s. It was part of a modern history series. The presenter was a historian who was born in the early seventies (too young to remember what it was really like, but old enough to have enjoyed the popular music and consumer products of the time and therefore have a distorted view). He was talking about the trials and tribulations of the decade. With a wry smile, he walked through a council housing estate built in the 1970s and described how the architectural conceptions of the time had led to the creation of ugly environments that had alienated the occupants and fostered crime and lawlessness. The vast expanses of concrete, influenced no doubt by what used to pass for 'modern art' had no plants, no trees, no displays of flowers; only a sterile geometry of brushed concrete and pebble dash. These spaces didn't seem belong to anyone; nobody felt responsible for them. In no time at all, they had been covered in graffiti, the estate was infested with criminal gangs and filled with 'problem' families.

Watching all this had quite an effect on me. I've often wondered why I have no fond memories of my early years as an adult. Well, that's not strictly true- I do have one fond memory of the 1970s. Here it is: In 1973, I was lying on top of the lovely Janice in the living room of her parent's house at 10:45 pm on a Saturday night. We had turned the volume of the television up so that our fumblings were drowned by Michael Parkinson who was interviewing George Best about football. This was followed by an interview with the man who played Ken Barlow in 'Coronation Street' although I think we'd finished by the time he came on.

As I watched the history program, it soon became clear to me that there was very little about the 1970s that was worth remembering and even less to remember fondly. Even my relationship with Janice ended in tears (mine) when she dumped me for someone else. Someone who had a bigger motorbike (that wasn't always breaking down like mine) and a proper job in a bank (and wasn't an impoverished student like me).

It had soon become painfully clear to me that it would be a very long time before I ever met such a beautiful and sexy girl again and for years I found it impossible to form any meaningful kind of relationship with any of the girls I did meet.

My time at university was spent in the library, studying; in the pub and then the disco on Saturday nights; and at the jazz club in Greenwich on Sunday lunchtimes. I was always a success in the pub and a failure in the disco. In pubs, I had a great affinity for alcohol of all kinds and could easily hold my own. In the disco, where it was assumed one might have a chance to dance with a girl or two, the loud music rendered me incapable of doing anything. I never met anyone who formed even a meaningless relationship with a girl he met at a disco. Robbed of the power of speech by deafening disco music, we'd ask girls to dance and then spend the next 3 minutes pretending we were enjoying ourselves. Even if we could have thought of something funny or amusing or interesting to say, it would have been drowned out by the music. Invariably, it all ended with a dreadful hangover the next day and not even a love bite to show for it.

The jazz club assembled at lunchtime at a cinema. In those days the matinee performances didn't start until 3:00pm. The club didn't have an alcohol licence, so you had to pay a couple of quid to get a plate of curry and rice and a 'Party Seven'of beer. 'Party Sevens' were huge cans of weak chemical beer that people only drank if there was nothing else left or nothing else available. Like many other aspects of life in the 1970s, Party Sevens are best forgotten. They are emblematic of the decade; they were the British Leyland of the world of beer; in the same league of naff '70s crap as platform shoes, Austin Allegro cars, space hoppers and the Bay City Rollers pop group. They were a symptom of the quiet desperation of a nation pretending to be happy while standards dropped and the national life and economy steadily declined.

If you'd like a vision of the 1970s by someone who once lived there, here it is: Imagine a man with a rope around his neck, standing on the gallows about to be executed. The priest tries to cheer him-up by wrapping tinsel around his neck and patting his bum with a 'fart' cushion as the trapdoor opens.

"Whoops-a-daisy"'

At student parties, around 11:30pm, when all the decent booze had gone, the drinkers turned, in desperation, to the unopened bottle of Martini or Dubonnet that one of the girls would have brought in a courageous attempt at sophistication. These were the kind of girls who wore skin-tight stain trousers that looked like they'd been sprayed onto their bodies with left-over paint just used to write grafitti on the walls of run-down housing estates. Like everything else in the 1970s that was actually desirable, such girls looked like they were available, but they never were, at least not to impoverished students like us. The way they dressed and the way they behaved were at a different level – like Jensen Interceptor cars and skiing holidays in the Swiss Alps, they were not for the likes of us.

In the 1970s, ordinary people hadn't yet discovered how to buy proper wine, let alone how to enjoy it and they returned from their holidays spent in places like Italy and Spain with the most tasteless green bottles filled with awful concoctions of sugary, sweet liquors drowning pieces of pickled fruit. These bottles would then be hidden away in sideboard cabinets, lurking in wait for hapless visitors and guests who would then be offered the stuff in a vain attempt at hospitality.

When even the Dry Martini was gone early on Sunday morning, desperate male partygoers would search for screwdrivers and penknives to open the Party Seven cans (by then we were all too drunk to find the can opener). Normally, the rest of the evening was a blur as the chemical beer mixed with everything else we had drunk that night to produce a toxic mix guaranteed to make the hangover last for most of Sunday.

One of the most remarkable differences between the 1970s and today is the difference in the prevalence and social acceptability of cigarette smoking. When I was a student, Universities provided ashtrays in the lecture theatres. It was considered polite to light-up in the middle of lectures - it showed you were paying attention. Pipe-smoking was common amongst older lecturers and Professors. They usually had yellow teeth and wore tweedy jackets with leather patches on the elbows. Younger lecturers smoked the same cigarettes as the students and were fairly indistinguishable from them in most other ways. They too, would think nothing of lighting up half way through the lecture. The 1970s was also the decade when people thought that their opinions were important and that everybody else needed to hear them. It was the height of political correctness to rage against the injustices of apartheid on Tuesday lunchtimes in the refectory, oblivious to the fact that everyone else wanted to talk about their exam results or where to find some decent beer. People used to protest against government 'cuts' without having any understanding of where governments got their money from and why there wasn't enough to fund government spending.

     I remember one occasion of particular vividness. I was sitting in the refectory at lunchtime with some friends and fellow students. We were eating cheese and pickle sandwiches and drinking instant coffee made of granules. The room was full of cigarette smoke and we were talking about our plans for the weekend. A friend of mine was explaining how he and his girlfriend were going to invite two other couples around to their flat for dinner on Saturday night. None of them knew how to cook or had any money to buy proper food, but they were planning to make mince and onions with some carrots and OXO cubes to add a bit of flavor. They had asked me how to cook mince and so, after explaining to them what a frying pan was and how to use it, I said "good luck" and that I hoped it would be all right on the night.

     "What did you just say?" asked a girl student sitting at an adjacent table, glaring at me with hatred.

     "Errrr....", I mumbled, "they're having some people round for dinner and I said I hoped it would be all right on the night?"

     "No you didn't!", she countered, accusingly.

     "You said...", she continued, glaring at me through henna-streaked ringlets of greasy hair, "you said, you hoped it would be all WHITE ON THE NIGHT!"

     "That's RACIST!"

     To the modern mind, to those of us accustomed to living in England in the 21st Century, it is almost inconceivable that anyone would misinterpret normal speech in this way or would subsequently react so strongly even if he or she did. However, we're talking about the 1970s: a time when there was a form of collective insanity that permeated the entire nation, bought on by inflation of 25% and by the appearance on television of ugly male politicians in grey suits, pretending to be working class.

Anyway, I suppose if I had been as quick-witted as many of the real racists around at the time, I would have stared back at her and said, calmly and quietly, as quick as a flash:

"Oh, I'm wee-ally soww-y you mis-heard me. I'm not a w-acist, I have a speech defect."

In fact, I said very little in explanation. Instead, I tried to turn the conversation around by talking about garlic (this was the 1970s, after all, and garlic was exotic, even dangerous)

One of the reasons I wasn't able to reply so cleverly to the girl student was because she was so ugly. Very quickly, I had realised that I was dealing with somebody who didn't care about how she looked or how she behaved or whether or not other people hated her guts. Her greasy hair was stained with henna, which contrasted with her white spotty face and wonky National Health teeth. She wore no make-up at all and was smoking hand-rolled cigarettes. She was wearing brown corduroy trousers and a scruffy orange tee-shirt with the words:

"AFRO-EURO-ASIATIC WOMEN'S COLLECTIVE AMALGAM" written on the front.

I knew then, as I know now, that it is pointless to try to appease such people. She obviously hated herself and clearly she wanted everyone else to hate her as well. With the benefit of hindsight, of course, the best way to respond would have been to tell her to fuck-off. The Anglo Saxon language still has its uses even in the modern world and this is a good example of how and when it can best be deployed most appropriately.

But I was young and polite and as I looked away from the ugly girl student, my eyes misted over and I felt a lump in my throat. For a moment, I couldn't speak at all.

I was overwhelmed by sadness and a deep sense of loss. I thought back to that fateful Saturday night the year before - the night when I went to heaven and back with an angel called Janice. We were in the living room lying on the floor, under soft lights. I was lying stark naked on top of her on a soft woolly carpet, kissing her lovely face, smelling her perfumed body, caressing her soft skin and telling her how much I loved her and how beautiful she was.

Well, that was then and this was now. Now, I was sitting in a smoky refectory, in a shitty part of London, crowded with scruffy, smelly students, eating crap food and being screamed at about racism by a zombie from hell.

The 1970s could be difficult at times.

Fortunately, these sad thoughts were soon dispelled by the re-appearance on the television of our friendly historian. He was walking down the High Street of some bloody awful London suburb, such as Tooting or Croydon, and talking about the failure of governments in the 1970s to deliver on consumer aspirations. The editing was very clever. As the presenter stopped walking, he grinned wickedly at the camera, which panned to the high street shops. As if by magic, the modern scene was replaced by real footage from the 1970s, taken from exactly the same spot. Modern cars with aerodynamic shapes, pleasing lines and tasteful colours were replaced by 1970s box-mobiles with chrome trimmings and "go-fast" stripes.

Cars in the 1970s were designed for people who didn't want to be envied and were painted in colors that blended with English towns on grey days in January. Grey and beige were popular colors for cars, but if you wanted to be really daring you could opt for olive green or even turmeric. People even had olive green bathroom suites.

On the television, we were shown 1970s housewives, walking down the street, dressed in pink overcoats and pulling wicker shopping baskets behind them. Their heads were covered with scarves to protect their permed hair-dos from the wind and rain. Men with Brylcreamed hair and donkey jackets walked past, with cigarettes dangling in their mouths, deftly side-stepping the dog shit on the pavement.

One of the enduring mysteries of the 1970s, something that confused us all at the time, has recently been solved:

"Why did dog shit change color when left on pavements for long periods of time?"

When dog turds landed on the pavement, they were normally brown or black. After a while, they went white. Why this happened was a complete mystery. It turns out that in order to increase profits, the dog food companies added finely ground chicken bones to dog food in order to add bulk and increase the weight. Apparently, the canine digestive system isn't particularly good at digesting bone. As the dog food traversed the canine gut, in a brown soup of enzymes and water, the nutrients were slowly absorbed, but the bone flour stayed where it was. Next, bacteria of all kinds got to work on what was left and the water was re-absorbed into the bloodstream. Only solids remained, including the ground-up chicken bones, which eventually saw daylight on the streets and pavements of English towns. In the 1970s, of course, dog owners thought that because dog physiology was natural, they could allow their dogs to defecate anywhere whenever nature called, which is why the UK in the 1970s was peppered with the stuff. It seems astonishing to the modern mind that it never occurred to local councils or anyone else that it was unpleasant or unhygienic to litter our public spaces with dog shit and that maybe someone should clean it up, or even better, that dog owners should take responsibility for their pets' turds in the same way they do their own. Anyway, nobody ever did clean it up, so the organic materials in the turd slowly leached away over time and the turd became increasingly dehydrated. Eventually, only the calcium from the chicken bones remained, leaving small white tubules on the pavement – the skeletal remains of Fido's lunch. When we were children, of course, we didn't really understand any of this and loved to kick skeletal dog turds and watch them explode into a cloud of dust. Oh, happy days!

"As inflation soared to 25%, housewives rushed to the supermarket to stock-up on daily necessities", announced our historian presenter, revelling in the awfulness of it all. The camera panned to the checkout of a local supermarket as tins of pork luncheon meat and packets of fish fingers were hastily lifted off the shelves and loaded into supermarket trollies by middle-aged housewives with blue hair and false teeth.

Back in the High Street, young girls in mini-skirts with stripy woolen tank-tops of rainbow colors stamped their feet against the cold, as they waited in long queues at the bus stop in the freezing rain. A young man with a sad expression on his face clomped into view. He was wearing black and white platform shoes, flared, satin jeans and a velvet jacket with huge lapels. An orange badge on one lapel indicated that he was a member of the 'Dennis the Menace' Fan Club. Around his neck was a long knitted scarf of many different colors, with frayed ends that trailed along the pavement on both sides. He puffed on a cigarette as the wind flapped his mullet hairstyle about his cheeks. He looked cold and miserable and seemed to be repeating the word "shit" to himself over and over and over and over again, in time with his unsteady footsteps.

At first I didn't recognise him.

Then I did.

"Oh, Christ", I thought. "It's me!"

You know you're getting old when you see yourself on television in a history programme

Day 19 The 1980s Come Back Disguised as a TV Series About Gardening

The ability to enjoy boring television programmes about gardening is a sure sign of the passing of the years. In fact, I've just recorded all of the six episodes of the most boring gardening programme of them all. It's called, 'The Victorian Kitchen Garden' and it's all about how the owners of large country houses used to grow their own fruit and vegetables in the Victorian era.

Just to make it really interesting, the producers found an old Victorian walled garden, in a derelict state and an old gardener to go with it. Anyway, the format of the show is to reconstruct a Victorian kitchen garden using the kinds of fruit and vegetables the Victorians would have used as well as authentic Victorian gardening techniques. If any of this sounds even remotely interesting, then it's a sure sign that you are old.

Starting in January, the team get to work with all the tasks would have been done in those far-off times.

The series was recorded in the 1980s, a decade known for the inoffensiveness of its soft furnishings, both domestic and commercial. Not unexpectedly, as the show starts, we are presented with a beige screen. The words:

'The Victorian Kitchen Garden'

written in nutty brown letters, form a friendly arch in the middle of the screen.

They had a liking for beige in the 1980s. People used to cover the walls of their houses with beige wallpaper, safe in the knowledge that almost any additional furniture or decorative item of almost any kind wouldn't clash with it. Beige was thought to be "safe" and such was the confidence of most people in their taste and sophistication, their houses were full of it. The owners didn't seem to mind, though. With beige you really were safe and you knew that nobody would laugh at you or accuse you of being a racist if you had a beige lounge suite. People even used to wear beige clothes. Beige corduroy trousers and a green pullover were a safe bet if you were going to a pub in a trendy part of London and didn't want people to ask you what newspaper you read.

Beige has the effect of stifling almost everything it comes into contact with. Maybe that's why the Job-Centres in those days were decorated with boring beige wallpaper and orange furniture. In many ways, the color beige sums up the strengths and weaknesses of the 1980s. The main strength of the 1980s was that it superseded the 1970s and the main weakness of the 1980s was that its failure to learn from the mistakes of the previous decade.

Returning to the Victorian Kitchen Garden and its opening sequence. A flute is playing in the background, extremely quietly and slowly. Our eyes are drawn to the words 'Victorian Kitchen Garden' interwoven with water-color sketches of all our favorite vegetables. We relax in front of the screen in quiet anticipation of whatever comes next.

Cut to a camera shot of a scruffy old brick wall with a patch of cabbages in front of it. Into the scene, from the left, strolls Peter, our presenter (a fully qualified horticulturalist and paid-up member of the ROYAL HORTICULTURAL SOCIETY).

"The Victorians grew a WIDE variety of produce in their WALLED kitchen gardens', he announces, gazing sternly at the camera.

The camera pans back from Peter's face and our attention is drawn to the fact that he is standing in front of a WALL. He is wearing a beige checked jacket, a cream shirt, a tie with brown and green stripes and brown trousers. The jacket has wide lapels and Peter's hair is of an uncertain length - somewhere in the no-man's-land between a 1970s mullet and a short back and sides. His tie is very wide and he has a black moustache. Peter stares, blankly, at the camera.

"Their AIM was to produce a steady supply of fresh fruit and vegetables during ALL THE SEASONS OF THE YEAR", he continues, helpfully.

Peter walks past a pile of manure. An old gardener (we are later to learn that this is Harry, our co-presenter) dressed in a tweed jacket, shirt and tie with waistcoat and moleskin trousers trudges around a pile of manure in his sturdy Wellington boots.

A flute plays softly in the background.

"Sometimes", continues Peter, "they would exhibit their produce at the ROYAL HORTICULTURAL SOCIETY in London!"

Cut to an old Victorian hall somewhere in London. It is filled with benches covered in carrots and parsnips. Groups of fat, old men with bald heads, red faces and false teeth are examining vegetables and giving them scores out of ten, which they write down in their brown notebooks. The atmosphere is very subdued and nobody in the hall is doing anything interesting. This is the 1980s, remember, the decade when the only people who were allowed to shout were alternative comedians and only then to cover up the fact that their jokes weren't funny.

Cutting back to Peter, he is sitting at a desk in an old library. The walls are covered with wood paneling and old books in various shades of beige and brown. He opens a small book and the camera pans to its title.

Proceedings of the Royal Horticultural Society 1853

"In 1853", states Peter, reading from the book, "The winner for the best carrots, with a score of NINETY FIVE PERCENT, was Mr. James Jeeves, head Gardener of Fairthorn Manor in Gloucestershire with a NEW VARIETY, cleverly named the ORANGE THRUSTER. This is a rare variety nowadays but there are still a few specimens left in the remaining WALLED KITCHEN GARDENS of Gloucestershire.

The camera pans to a walled kitchen garden somewhere in Gloucestershire. A flute plays slowly and quietly in the background and the camera pans across a bed of carrot tops and green leaves.

"All this gardening required a STEADY SUPPLY of nutrients", says Peter, appearing from the right and coming to a stop in front of a rusty old oil drum full of dirty rainwater.

"Nothing was ever THROWN AWAY", he continues looking sternly at the camera. Although Peter is obviously very knowledgeable and well-meaning, you do get the feeling that he is telling us off for not starting up our own compost heap with potato peelings and spent tea bags. It soon becomes clear, though, that Peter has a better idea.

"Luckily, there was plenty of fertiliser to be had, if you knew where to look. Earlier today, Harry and I sent ALISON out into the sheep pasture, to find some manure for HARRY's new cauliflower patch".

Alison, it transpires, is a trainee horticulturalist (soon to be a member of the ROYAL HORTICULTURAL SOCIETY in London, we expect). Alison is a modest and attractive young woman wearing Wellington boots, blue jeans a blue jumper and no make-up (she is a trainee horticulturalist, remember - she is appearing on television for the first time and is someone to be taken seriously. She is not to be subjected to lewd comments or sexist remarks by any of the viewers, by men in general or by younger versions of men like me, in particular).

Where all this political correctness and gender neutrality falls down of course is that Alison has the most gorgeous 1980s hair style. This is the kind of hair style that still has a tremendous impact on men of my age, conjuring-up images of girls with 'big' hair wearing yellow polka dot jackets with huge, padded shoulders, tight-fitting pencil skirts, high heeled sandals, bright red toenails, huge earrings, gold ankle chains and tons and tons and tons of sexy make-up and perfume. Almost immediately, Peter's voice fades into the background and I imagine a young version of me popping out to the field with Alison to give her a helping hand in the hope of luring her into the potting sheds afterwards to talk about parsnips, our senses bombarded by the earthy smells of compost and potting soil.

Back to nature!

Unfortunately, my dreams of taking the slow train to paradise with Alison are soon shattered as Peter holds a sack in front of the camera and announces gleefully:

"This hession sack is like a giant teabag full of MANURE!"

He lowers the sack into a barrel of rainwater. Rainwater, the color of diarrohea, drips out into the barrel.

"We have soaked the MANURE for a week and now it is ready to be used as a LIQUID FEED on the cauliflower patch". Harry appears pushing an old trolley with a container on it. He fills the container with shitty rainwater and pushes-off in the general direction of the cauliflowers.

"The gardeners of old always used to say that you knew it was ready for use when it was the colour of tea", explains Harry, helpfully, as if this were something we might want to try ourselves.

The camera cuts to Peter walking purposefully towards a bed of cauliflowers.

"HEAD GARDENERS in Victorian WALLED GARDENS", continues Peter, "prided themselves on their ability to produce a FRESH CAULIFLOWER at any time of the year. WOE BETIDE the gardener who was unable to do so". Harry is dutifully dousing the cauliflowers with shitty rainwater – now we understand why.

Alison appears next with a basketful of cowpats that she has collected from the pasture. She looks very shy and timid and, understandably, does not seem to be very happy. Clearly, she is being given all the worst jobs. Because she is a trainee horticulturalist, she has to work from the bottom-up, I suppose. Literally. This is why she has been sent trudging through muddy fields in the freezing cold with a basket to collect cow shit.

For a moment, I feel sad, I regret that I wasn't there at the time. If I had been, I could have made Alison happy, I'm sure. We could have had a friendly chat in the pub over a pint or two. You never know, there might have been a nice dry barn nearby with some straw in it. We could have gone there to take shelter from the rain, y'know, talk about stuff and get to know each other a bit better, in the way that young people do.

We'll never know, will we, because now, both Alison and I are far too old.

It's all too much for me, you know, it really is. What with Peter's boring voice droning on and on in a relentless MONOTONE, Alison's big hair, the giant teabag full of shit and that blasted flute constantly droning on and on in the background, I have now been completely hypnotised.

I have to know what is going to happen next. Will the cardoons be ready in time? What is the secret behind a firm parsnip and how will Harry's cobnuts take to a good, hard pruning? Inevitably, I record the entire series and watch the lot, on a rainy Sunday, all in one go. Time stands still and even though it's boring, there is something comforting about the way it has been made and presented.

There is only one other television programme that is as boring as this one with similar hypnotic effects. That, of course, is the teletubbies, which you can watch for hours: all the higher centres of your brain will shut down and time will seem to stand still. You don't believe me? Google 'Teletubbies man in house sketch' and watch the sequence. I am sure many young children were permanently traumatised by it. Instead of bringing back hanging, all murderers and terrorist suspects should be locked in to a cell for 24 hours a day with this sketch running in a constant loop. That'll teach them a lesson!

The government seems to think that there is a problem with the ageing workforce and that we must all work longer. I have the answer. The Victorian Kitchen Garden program must be made compulsory viewing in all the old people's homes the length and breadth of the land. We'll paint the walls of these homes beige and give the old people orange chairs to sit in and tins of Party Seven beer to drink. We'll hypnotise the old bastards, kit them out in overalls and Wellingtons and then put them to work in walled gardens, which they can never leave. If they complain, we'll tell them it's the 1980s and they're still young. If they refuse to work, we'll lock them in a beige room with nothing to eat but pork luncheon meat, digestive biscuits and the teletubbies 'man in house' sketch repeating endlessly in the background.

Day 18 Watch with Mother

The 1990s marked a major and unforgettable change in my life. My kids were born in the early 1990s and I spent the next few years covered in snot and strawberry jam. We won't say anything about what came out of the other end. I volunteered to be chief cook and bottlewasher and while my wife handled the sanitary end of things.

I was watching a movie on the TV the other day and I tried to guess when it was made.

"It can't be that old", I thought. Everyone was smartly dressed stylishly with short hair and all the girls looked nice. There were computers on the desk, there were printers in the offices, the furniture looked modern and the men wore smart suits.

No cellphones, though.

You start to realise you are old when 1991 looks modern and the fashions look cool.

The 1990s was the decade when I converted from bachelor to husband and dad. I remember the fun and excitement of being a dad for the first time.

One of the most rewarding things about being a Dad is that you can revert to childhood yourself and do and say all sorts of silly things to make your children laugh. It is their sense of fun and capacity for spontaneous humour that makes playing with kids so enjoyable.

It wasn't long before I started making up bedtime stories to help them get to sleep. The only problem was that the stories made them laugh so much they didn't feel sleepy any more.

I remember three stories in particular:

Eusebius the Frog goes Shopping

Eusebius the Frog goes on Holiday

AND

Eusebius the Frog gets abducted by Aliens and founds a Race of Hyper-intelligent Super-beings on the Planet ZorG.

Eusebius the Frog goes Shopping was their favourite, of course. I can still remember the story.

1. Once upon a time, there was a frog called 'Eusebius'

Now, Eusebius is a very funny name, but Eusebius was a very funny frog

2. Eusebius lived in a small, muddy pond at the end of the High St in a small country town.

The name of the town was 'Townlet'. It was called Townlet because:

1. It was a town
2. 2. It was small
3. That was its name

At one of the high street was the frogpond.

And at the other end, there was a SOOOOOOPermarket, where the people who lived in the town could go by things that they needed.

In the SOOOOOpermarket, all manner of things were on sale.
One of the main differences between the frogpond and the SOOOOOpermarket was that there was nothing for sale in the frogpond.

But there were lots of flies and creepy crawlies, there was pondweed and there was green pondwater that tasted of mud.

And there were even shopping trolleys that had been thrown into the pond by Hooligans and Ne'er do Wells.

3. One day, Eusebius was having some elevenses with his best friend, Tiberius, the toad.

Tiberius took a sip of pod water and looked at Eusebius.

'Why's your name called Eusebius?' asked Tiberius

Eusebius looked back at Tiberius and wondered whether toads were really as silly as people said they were.

4. 'My names not called 'Eusebius', said Eusebius, 'Eusebius is my name because that's what I'm called'.

'So if you're called Eusebius, what's your name called?' asked Tiberius.

'My name's not called anything', replied Eusebius. 'Names don't have names, only frogs have names'

'And toads', replied Tiberius

5. Eusebius decided that frogs were definitely more intelligent than toads and hopped away for a spot of lunch.

6. He found a nice water lilly leaf, floating in the middle of the pond and he hopped out of the water onto it.

A crunchy fly, buzzled past and Eusebius caught it with his tongue.

'CRRRUNCHHH!

7. Then he dived into the pond, all the way down to the bottom, where he found a nice thick piece of green pondweed.

Eusebius took a bite of pondweed and chewed it 15 times, because he was a good frog and his mother had always told him not to rush his food and to always eat his greens.

7. Back on the lilly pad, it had started to rain.

Eusebius looked around him at the muddy pond, as large drops of rain gollolloped down, throwing glossy drops of green pondwater splashing into the air.

8. Eusebius was bored.

     'Rainy days are always boring', he thought. 'All the creepy crawlies hide away in nooks and crannies, the flies can't fly and there's nothing for me to do, no crunchy flies to eat and no creepy crawlies to chase.

9. Eusebius decided to go shopping.

10. He hopped off the lilly pad and swam to the banks of the pond, up the grassy bank, past the shopping trollies and onto the High St.

11. First, he came to a bakery, but frogs don't eat Bakewell Tarts or Eccles cakes and they don't like bread or Cornish pasties.

So, he hopped away to the next shop.

12. He liked the smell of the fish at the fishmongers, but all the fish on sale were far too big for him to carry, let alone to eat. Besides, there were plenty of little fish in his pond. Fish like sticklebacks that are small and tasty. Fish that frogs can catch for free.

13. Then he hopped past the Delicatessen and looked at all the strange and exotic food on sale.

'It looks so nice!', he thought. 'But, I'd better not go in, otherwise they might put me up for sale as well!' He thought, as he spotted a tin of frog's legs in gravy.

14. Next, he arrived at the Soooopermarket.

'This looks good!, thought Eusebius, reading a sign on the Soooopermarket window that said:

'Two for the price of one deals! New customers welcome, including frogs.'

15. So Eusebius grabbed a shopping trolly and hopped into the Soooopermarket. First he arrived at the fizzy drinks section.

There was cherryade and lemonade and limeade and cream soda and there was something specially for frogs – fizzy cheese and onion drink.

So, Eusebius picked-up a bottle and put it in his trolley.

16. Next, he came to the ice cream section. There was cheery chocolate vanilla ice cream, there was toffee and caramel ice cream and there was even chocolate chip cookee ice cream. Eusebius didn't like the look of any of these and was he was about to leave when all of sudden, in a dark corner of the ice cream cabinet, he saw a small tub of garlic and cabbage ice cream.

17.   'Wow!', thought Eusebius, 'that looks tasty.'

As he picked up the tub and put it into his trolley, he noticed a sign.

'Special Offer – half price for all Frogs when you present your identification at the checkout'.

Luckily, Eusebius had bought his driving licence with him, so he could prove that he was a frog.

18. Next, Eusebius came to the cake section.

There was cheesecake and there was chocolate cake and there were cakes with hundreds and thousands on. As he hopped past, Eusebius noticed a small packet of white and green coloured cakes.

'My favourites!', he exclaimed. 'Radish and celery cakes, Yum, Yum!'

19. Eusebius was looking forward to a feast back at the pond. As he sped towards the checkout, he went passed the crisps section. There were cheese and onion flavour crisps, salt and vinegar flavour, barbecue chicken flavour and, in the corner, in a brown and yellow packet......newt and pondweed flavoured crisps.

'Bet they taste nicer than flies', thought Eusebius, grabbing a packet.

20. He soon arrived back to the pond, loaded with bags full of food that frogs find delicious.

There was a funny hopping sound behind him. It was Tiberius.

'Hello Eusebius', said Tiberius. 'What have you been doing?'

'I've been shopping', replied Eusebius.

'And what are all those things called?' asked Tiberius

'They're called 'groceries'' replied Eusebius, 'But that's not their name.'

Tiberius thought about this for a while but didn't really understand what Eusebius meant. He soon cheered-up though, when Eusebius gave him a glass of fizzy onion drink and a piece of radish and celery cake for his afternoon tea.

The End

Having kids in the 90s was great - computer games supplemented bedtime stories and we all had fun learning to play the Tarzan jungle game on our home pc. My kids grew-up inside the internet, which is a main part of the generation gap that divides us. Do you remember the early home internet and all the funny noises it used to make as you went online?
    I went to exchange my old cellphone the other day. A very young shop assistant took my old Blackberry-style phone and replaced it with a smartphone. Do you know what she said?
    "Wow - real buttons! I've seen pictures of these but I've never used one."
    I suppose one of the differences between being an ageing parent today and an ageing parent 50 years ago is that technology changes so fast. The 1990s weren't yesterday in technological terms, but they were a long, long time ago: before Facebook, before Google and before a lot of other things we now take for

granted. In their own way there was something different from my own childhood.

Of course, none of this answers the question that any parent or grandparent of a certain age will ask:

'What's happened to all the snot these days?"

Maybe I should look it up on the internet?

Day 17: Remembering The Noughties

One of the more memorable occasions in the early years of the 2000s happened around the time I took a renewed interest in my health and fitness.

It was early on a Tuesday morning in February 2003 and I was standing in front of the bathroom mirror shaving as I got ready to go to work.

All of a sudden, a rude voice shouted at me from the bedroom.

It was my wife.

'You're fat!' she shouted.

This was memorable for three reasons. Firstly, I had not been expecting it. Secondly, it felt like having ice-cold vinegar squirted into my ear. Thirdly, it was true.

I stopped shaving and looked at myself in the mirror. My initial impulse was to offer excuses and pull my tummy in. Her timing was perfect though. There, standing in front of the mirror looking at myself, I knew she was right.

I was not the man I used to be.

I was the kind of middle-aged man I had always felt superior to and laughed at.

I had turned into Mr. Potato Man.

Mr. Potato Men are often seen on the beaches of English seaside towns on rare sunny days in August. The kind of days that the tabloid press reports on the front page, boasting that it is hotter in Margate than the Costa del Sol. Such men are also seen on holiday on Spain where all the Europeans laugh at them with their fish and chips, warm beer, and football shirts. They are the kind of men who wear socks inside their sandals. They are the kind of men whose wives take a bottle of rose wine along when they go to the beach, drink it with lunch and then pass-out around 2:45 in the afternoon, waking-up on a stretcher a few hours later, on the way to hospital with sunburn and dehydration.

Mr. Potato Men have large tummies, skinny legs and knobbly knees. They have rounded, sloping shoulders and they often have a bald patch. One of the defining features of Mr. Potato Men is that their stomachs are completely out of proportion to the rest of their bodies.

I hated myself and felt disgusted.

"Never mind", said my wife cheerfully. 'You can go on a diet. I'll do it with you.'

Aren't women nice?

Anyway, I got dressed for work and looked at myself in the mirror again before I left. Just checking, you know. Maybe I didn't look so fat wearing a nice smart suit.

More denial?

In fact, I looked just like a middle-aged Mr. Potato Man who has just bought a suit from Marks and Spencers that has been specifically designed for fat Mr. Potato Men like him who are in denial.

Denial is not just a river in Africa.

Well, there was no way out. I bought a book about the Atkins diet and over the next week read it from cover to cover. Being a mad scientist, by trade I understood what Atkins was talking about without believing a word of it. How can you lose weight by eating large quantities of protein and fat, putting cream in your tea and coffee instead of low fat milk and eating meat or fish with practically every meal?

It didn't make sense.

When I finished the book, I made a diet plan for two to last two weeks of the diet ("Stage 1"). I could not imagine what it would be like to go without alcohol, caffeinated drinks, sugary or starchy foods (bread and potatoes) for two weeks. Anyway, it went something like this.

Day 1: Start the day with a three-egg omlette cooked in butter, with ham, cheese and mushrooms and half a raw tomato. Lunch was a Greek salad with a cold chicken leg and dinner was salmon cooked in butter with a cream sauce and a handful of asparagus.

Decaffeinated tea or coffee were allowed with cream (milk was banned) and no sugar

Day 2: Similar to day 1 but with cheeses and salad for lunch and a lamb chop, turnip and tomato for dinner

Day 3: By day 3, I was starting to feel a little weak. Atkins warns you about this and points out that you might get out of breath walking up the stairs. Apparently it happens because your body has been starved of carbohydrates and you will have used up all the stored carbohydrates in your muscles and liver. The result is that your metabolism has to re-calibrate and draw on an alternative source of energy – fat. The Atkins diet being what it is, there is plenty to draw on, so by days 4 and 5, the feeling of weakness had passed and I started to notice a rapid loss of weight.

Day 6: I weighed myself and had lost about 3 kilograms. I was using a new notch on my belt to hold my trousers up and started to feel better. The diet is boring and tiresome, but the rapid loss of weight was very rewarding. By day 10 I started to notice big changes and by day 14 – the end of Stage 1, I had lost 5 kilograms. Lying in the bath that evening, I looked down at my stomach – it was flat as a pancake, no more Mr Potatoe Man, no more man boobs.

My wife, unfortunately, only lost 1.5 kilograms and was very disappointed. I explained to her that Atkins does discuss this in his book – some people just don't respond to low carbohydrate diets very well.

Anyway, I then progressed to Stage 2 of the diet and my wife switched to calorie counting, which works for her. Stage 2 is like Stage 1 with the added luxury of a handful of nuts as a mid-morning snack and a slice of carrot or spoonful of peas with the other main meals. The real highlight of stage 2 is that you can drink alcohol (low carbohydrate options such as gin and diet tonic are allowed, whereas milk stout isn't. I could live with that).

After 3 months, I had lost 8 kilograms and thrown away a perfectly good suit because it was large in all the wrong places. On the plus side, the suit I got married in in 1991 was a perfect fit again (although the style was a little dated).

What are we to make of this? It turns out that, like most things in the 1970s, the dietary advice we were given was completely wrong. Going back to the 1960s, the advice was very similar to that of today – don't eat too much starchy food, watch the bread and potatoes and fill-up with leafy vegetables. I remember watching Michael Caine in the movies 'Alfie'. His girlfriend cooks him traditional English food with puddings like jam roly-poly and custard and he tells her off for making him eat 'stuff that blows you out'.

Well, starchy food does 'blow you out' it seems. The meat industry uses starch as a cheap way of fattening up cattle and a starchy diet causes many people to retain water (three moleculles of water for every molecule of glycogen, aooarently). That is why I lost so much weight so quickly on Atkins, the first few kilograms of weight loss aren't fat – they're fluid.

In some ways, the dietary advice given in the 1970s wasn't exactly wrong, it was just overtaken by economic events. With increasing affluence people had more money to spend on food and spend it they did. Back in the 1930s when most people had less disposable income, fatty and starchy food was common but back then many people had only one cooked meal per day – bread or porridge for breakfast, a cooked lunch and a sandwich or beans on toast for tea. No wonder they weren't fat.

One of the most remarkable and unexpected things about the Atkins diet (or low carbohyrate diets in general) is that you don't feel hungry. This is because, with practically no carbohydrate in your food, the body has to make the glucose needed by the brain. This has to happen all the time, so your blood glucose level is low and doesn't fluctuate very much. These fluctuations are one of the cues for hunger. An empty stomach is another such cue and so when you eat meals high in fat and protein they take longer to digest and you feel fuller for longer.

Starchy foods are the opposite of course and with hindsight we can see what has happened over the last 40 years. People have been told to avoid fatty foods and have eaten starchy and sugary foods instead, they now feel hungry every few hours and have the money to buy expensive snacks and treats.

The diet was a life-changing experience. I learnt some useful lessons about food and nutrition that I have stuck with ever since and my weight has remained the same – thanks Dr. Atkins. My wife was pleased that I had lost weight and that my appearance had improved. I started to buy new clothes, with a younger, slimmer look, more in keeping with times. One day, I was getting dressed before taking my wife out for the evening. Standing in front of the wardrobe mirror, I heard that voice again, like ice-cold vinegar being squirted into my ear.

'You're vain!'

'Stop looking at yourself in the mirror!'

You can't win, you just can't.

Day 16: 2000 and Teens

There is nothing more likely to induce stress and worry in the mind of a middle-aged Dad than the plaintiff cry of a teenage daughter in need of money.

We were cruising the Caribbean and were trudging through the jungle on a Caribbean island on a day trip and adventure break, zip-wiring through the canopy. It was great fun, of course, the trees looked very nice and the jungle wasn't too smelly. It was even more fun to watch all the ageing mums and dads flinging themselves onto a rope and swinging Tarzan-like over a net onto a rope ladder suspended from a tree about 10 metres away. Healthy and fit young islanders, our guides and coaches, shouted helpful encouragement as the safety lines snagged and another ageing parent plunged into the abyss.

The teenagers, not only mine but everyone else's it seemed, were invariably successful, except when they didn't want to be and felt like impersonating their Mums and Dads. I must say, the impersonations of wobbly jelly grannies plunging like blobs of pink blancmange into the safety net were rather amusing. One teenage boy pretended to be a skinny old grandad, dropping through the canopy like an octopus falling out of a tree.

Anyway, after a day of jolly japes and fun in the forest canopy, we all trudged back to meet the bus that was to return us to our cruise ship. The parents led the way and the teenagers lagged behind, in the way that teenagers do.

'Daa----ad!', came a squeaky voice from behind.

I froze and stopped dead in my tracks.

'Yes!' I growled defensively, only to be elbowed in the ribs by my wife.

'Wrong Dad!" she laughed. "Daniella's over there, not behind us. Don't you know where your DAUGHTER is? We ARE in the middle of the jungle you know and you don't know where she is, do you? What kind of father are you anyway, that's what I'd like to know? What are you going to do if she gets LOST and we're LATE getting back? And WHY can't you tell that the accent was American? Can't you tell the difference between an American and English accent even when it's your own DAUGHTER, hmmm?"

Despite this barrage of questions, I breathed a silent sigh of relief.
My wallet was safe for now.
My wife summed it quite succinctly.
'A man of your age. I don't know'.

Have you ever noticed that after you marry them, women start to ask you multiple questions all in one go, whereas they never used to do this when you were dating them?

I wonder why it is? Do you think it might be because when you were dating them, they were saving-up all the questions for later? Or is it because women think differently from men? I've never really believed all this talk about 'Men are from Mars and Women are from Venus', or that we do think differently. Women are supposed to be good at multi-tasking and bad at reading maps while men are good at visual-spatial reasoning and maths?

That's the theory anyway, but my wife, for example, is excellent at reading maps and at navigation in general, particularly when we are on holiday in a strange town, I am driving and there is a shopping centre nearby. She is, as you will have guessed, a much better and safer driver than I am, which explains why she always asks me to drive when we go out.

Or does it? In any case, I do think that wives think differently from husbands though.

These thoughts were going through my mind when we got back to ship and it was then that I did eventually get 'Dadded' and this time by my real daughter.

Fortunately, she was not asking for money. She had been bitten by mosquitos in the jungle and was covered in itchy spots.

Panic over.

So we took her to the ship's medical centre where they smothered her in cream free of charge thanks to the ship's on board health service. After that, we took her to the lounge and filled her up with donuts and ice cream, courtesy of our all-inclusive cruise package.

Another lucky escape for Dad's wallet!

Happy days!

Day 15: An Appointment with Doctor Wendy

I decided it was time to visit Dr Wendy to discuss a sensitive topic. This is one of those topics that is sensitive for a man of any age, but it is painfully sensitive for a man who is only just beginning to realise that he is old.

I'm talking of course about the deployability problem. Most men will remember sitting on the top deck of the bus on the way home from school when they were about 15 years of age. Arriving at your stop, you'd thrust your hands into your pockets, and hobble, hunched over and head down, for the exit, hoping that nobody would notice the enormous erection that had appeared five minutes before for absolutely no reason whatsoever.

Those days are long gone, of course and it was with fond memories of past experiences and lingering regrets about missed opportunities that I found myself in the waiting room for my three o'clock appointment with Dr Wendy.

I would, of course, have preferred a discussion with a male doctor, preferably an old male doctor who has been through it all himself. Men are not known for their empathy when it comes to matters of an emotional nature. However, and many women might be surprised by this, they have extremely good empathy when it comes to matters physical. We all know what it must feel like to not to be able to deliver the goods on time.

Dr. Wendy, of course, hasn't got any empathy at all, for men or women, particularly if they are patients of hers and they don't feel well. She is not the best person to talk to about health problems in particular and well-being in general. She is about 63 years of age, overweight with a dumpling-like figure and a frumpy nature. Her taste in clothing brings back memories of the fabrics used to upholster living room furniture in 1970s. It looks like it's been specially designed to make stains of all kinds disappear. I was watching a television about Ancient Greece the other day. Spartan warriors went into battle wearing red cloaks so that if they were injured, the blood wouldn't show. God knows what Dr. Wendy is trying to cover up by wearing the clothes that she does, but whatever it is, I feel sorry for the patients who donated it.

One of the benefits of getting old is that you less inquisitive and can't be bothered with all the frilly-knickered nonsense that we have to put up with in the modern world.

I walked into the consulting room and Dr. Wendy looked up at me from behind her desk. For a moment, the thought crossed my mind that I couldn't care less if I never had another erection ever again. That's the effect Dr. Wendy has on people, particularly men and even more so if they are patients of hers. I think Dr. Wendy would be better-deployed working for an international development agency. They should pack her off to care for people in poor, overpopulated places like India. Birth rates would plummet. Five minutes in the care of Dr. Wendy is enough to put anyone off sex.

Every cloud has a silver lining, I suppose and I consoled myself with the thought that if Dr Wendy wanted to examine me, there was no chance whatsoever that I would be embarrassed by a spontaneous erection.

Dr. Wendy has a view on the ageing process – it's all my own fault. I may be 59 years of age, but if I had looked after myself better, I'd still be 33, going out to work and digging the garden, living a healthy life and not cluttering-up her surgery with my trivial health problems, that are all my own fault anyway and nothing to do with her.

She beckoned me to take a seat.

'What seems to be the trouble?' she asked, impatiently.

'Well, it's rather personal', I began.

'Most health problems are', she replied helpfully. 'Go on', she said, looking at me as if I was a 5-year old who'd just wet his pants at the school assembly and left a puddle on the laminated floor of the school hall.

I explained that recently I had noticed that I was not quite the man I used to be in a rather personal way and that I was having difficulty rising to the occasion.

'Yes, well that's normal in a man of your age, particularly if you drink too much and don't get enough exercise'. 'Ah, well…', I replied.

She took my blood pressure, checked my pulse and weighed me and made a few notes.

I knew what was coming.

'Nothing wrong with you!' she declared reproachfully.

I know, I know, it's all my own fault.

Day 14: What the Experts Say About Ageing

I was reading a report published by the UK's Health and Safety Executive the other day. The report was all about the employment of older workers and what employees needed to know in order to cope.

According to the HSE, an 'older' worker is someone over 50 years of age.

Well, that's that then, isn't it? I'm old and useless and it's official.

The writers of the report put it this way:

In the UK, there were 20.7 million people 50 years or older in 2007, which is a 50% increase since 1951. This increase in older age groups is projected to continue. Similarly, the percentage of people employed in 2009 who are of Statutory Pension Age (SPA) or older has increased from 8% to 12%. Life expectancy has risen between 2000 and 2005 and is projected to continue rising. It is suggested that men at 65 could now expect to live a further 12.8 years in good or fairly good health and women could live for a further 14.5 years.

Isn't that absolutely fab? Not only am I now, and this is official, an 'older' worker, but I can carry on being an older worker and carry on working with lots of other miserable old bastards for many years to come.

What advice does the HSE have for people who want to employ 'older' workers, like me?

First, it points out rather helpfully, that there is *'no consistent evidence'* that older workers are generally less productive than younger workers.

You have no idea how wonderful that makes me feel. But what about the inconsistent evidence?

It then says that part of the reason for this is that most *jobs don't require people to work at full capacity.* Implying, of course, that older people have lower capacity to work or that older workers are just as lazy as younger workers, so age doesn't matter.

I wonder how old the top management of the HSE really is? I suspect that they themselves are old and it sounds to me like they want to keep their jobs.

What I want to know is this. Before the boffins at the HSE published this report, did any of them, even one, actually speak to any 'older' workers and ask them what they thought? Did it ever to occur to them that any of the people reading this report (which was intended for employers) might also fall into the category of 'older worker', given the statistics used at the beginning of the report about the increasing proportion of older people? In other words, the HSE has just told the ageing senior managers of all our large organisations that they can carrying making the same mistakes as they have done in the past and that there is no reason at all why they should be replaced.

If the HSE had its way, everyone over 60 would automatically qualify for a free pass to the disabled toilets.

Day 13: I Decide on All the Things I Don't Want to do Before I die

Swimming with Dolphins.

I don't want to go swimming with dolphins. I know that they are not fish. They are mammals and they live in the sea, except the ones that live in rivers and get eaten by the Chinese. People say that they are intelligent but I don't believe this for a moment. I think that if they were intelligent, they would have moved on, you know, made an effort and done something creative or useful. All they seem to do is swim around in the sea all day eating fish and making squeaky clicking noises.

Now, some people say that there are many kinds of intelligence. This, of course, is utter rubbish and is just a way of covering up the fact that dolphins are stupid and don't do anything useful.

What on Earth would be the point of spending your time in the sea surrounded by a bunch of stupid sea mammals that look like fish and keep bumping into you when you're trying to have a decent swim? I suppose I could go to China and try some dolphin steak for lunch, but quite honestly, I can't be bothered and I expect it would be totally uninteresting and complete waste of time and money.

The fact is, even if they WERE fish, I still wouldn't want to swim with them. We all know what fish get up to in the sea and don't suppose that dolphins are any better even if they are intelligent, which they're not.

Hire a Beach Hut in Dorset and take a Holiday in England for a Change

Can you imagine? Sitting in a drafty, wooden shed by the sea in August, listening to the weather forecast on the radio:

"…and the weather today will be rain, followed by showers, becoming stormy later".

Beach huts don't have proper services like electricity or gas and you're not supposed to sleep in them overnight. Imagine how horrible it would be if you did? Waking up at 7:30 in the morning after a restless night listening to the rain on the corrugated iron roof. You light the gas primer stove to boil water to make tea and it takes forever as the stainless steel kettle sucks the life out of the weak, blue flame. The whistle on the kettle eventually sounds in the way that camping kettles do – weakly and with no enthusiasm, like a vicar at a strip club when the lap dancer tells him it's his turn.

After tea and a bowl of cold porridge you decide to go for a bracing walk along the beach. The slate-splashed sea merges with the dull grey clouds and you search in vain for the horizon, peering between windy gusts, with rain-slapped cheeks. Soggy droplets plop-off your chin and down your shirt onto your chest, finding their way into places you'd rather not be reminded about.

After walking for an hour or two, you are now thoroughly depressed, cold, wet and bored. Returning to the hut, you dry yourself, wrap a blanket around your shoulders and turn the radio on.

"And the weather in Alicante today is fine, with clear blue skies and a high of 29 degrees. A light breeze will arrive later in the day and the sea temperature is a comfortable 24 degrees".

I mean, really!

Bungy-jumping

I think there is something wrong with some people, you know. I mean who on earth would want to fling themselves off a tall building or bridge only to be saved from certain death by a couple of elastic ropes? I have heard that it is particularly dangerous for old people to attempt bungy jumping. The reason is that you fall head first and which causes a momentary loss of blood in the brain. As the elastic cords start to stretch and decelerate the body, the body slows down but the blood doesn't and the result is a rush of blood to the head that can cause a blood vessel to burst with serious consequences.

Looking on the bright side, there might be a germ of an idea here for dealing with our ageing population. After lulling them into a sense of security in WALLED gardens and playing the teletubbies MAN IN THE HOUSE sketch over and over again, we could take them bungy jumping. We could use special non-elastic ropes that cause rapid deceleration of the body thereby maximising the chances of a brain injury leading to death.

Like all good ideas though, there's a catch. Our old friends at the Health and Safety Executive would have none of it. There'd be endless inspections and tests, safety audits and HAZARD IDENTIFICATION EXERCISES.

I suppose successful ageing is really just one long HAZARD IDENTIFICATION EXERCISE. You can't stop the solids hitting the fan but you can run for cover if you know it's going to happen.

Join a Rambler's Club and Go for Walks in the Local Countryside

There's nothing like the English countryside is there?

Rambling is very popular with certain kinds of old people. Normally people with more time than money and a love for cheese and pickle sandwiches. I've seen them gathering in small groups with their raincoats and hiking boots and backpacks and thermos flasks. They disappear into the woods with their compasses and maps and books entitled 'Fungal Growths and How to Spot the Edible Ones'.

I wonder what they get up to all day?

Have you ever noticed that when people stand on hill admiring a lovely view they always take a deep breath and tip the head back.

Why?

I read an interesting theory about this the other day. Apparently our ability to pay attention to what we are doing is limited and after using to for a while, we use it up and have to do nothing for a while to replenish ourselves.

It's all based on the idea that self-control is like a muscle and it depends on the levels of glucose in our brains. So, when we have to exert self-control (like explaining to a teenage daughter why you are not going to give her any money) we use it up and need to have a rest. Teenage daughters, of course, have an uncanny ability to tax our self-control resources to the limit. There's 'emotional dissonance' (you want to thump them for using bad language and being disrespectful but have to stay calm and diplomatic for example, or they have their nose pierced and you have to pretend it looks cool rather than ridiculous). There's 'overcoming inner resistance' (you don't want to stay up late to collect them from a party but you have to and so you stay at home and watch programmes about people making cakes badly, resist the urge to drink beer and arrive at the agreed time only to have to wait for half an hour as the undrunk beer you left on the kitchen table slowly goes flat and warm). Then there's 'resisting distraction'. You are trying to watch a fascinating programme about financial crises and their implications for household budgets and you daughter and her friends are sitting in the lounge talking about boys and make up. On the one hand, you know that it's none of your business and the kind of situation where Dad's should just shut-up and behave themselves. On the other hand, your attention gets captured by the odd 'trigger word' – words that Dad's respond to automatically when uttered by teenage daughters. 'Sex' is one such word of course, as are 'boys', 'parties' and 'sleepover'. 'Impulse control' is the last attentional challenge we have to deal with. After having a potentially convivial, if fairly solitary Saturday night ruined by taxi duties, the depleted Dad delivers the teenage daughter home and then has to resist the urge to get back on the drinking schedule and catch-up. This is fatal, of course, because although it might be fun at the time, it invariably ruins most of Sunday and is not worth the effort when you are old. Younger people might be able to get away with it though.

So, where does this leave us in relation to rambling? I think these ramblers are all depleted. The theory states that walks in the woods are restorative because there are no demands on attention from outside. There are plenty of things to look at in the woods but it's not like going shopping where you have to pay attention to what you are doing and how much things cost. So, when tramping through the bluebells, our attention might be captured, in a pleasant way, by the sight of fungal growths such as "Oakley's Lesser-Spotted Puffball" but there's no requirement to look at it.

Is rambling the answer? I'm not sure, you could just pour a beer and go channel surfing through cookery programmes, while looking at the food and learning nothing about cooking. With a bit of luck, you might come across the Teletubbies 'MAN IN THE HOUSE SKETCH' which only demands the attentional capacity of two-year old.

Give up Booze for Lent

This is something that I have done already and have no intention of ever doing again. The reason for this is very simple.

It is unutterably tedious and dull.

Every minute of every day seems like 10:30 on a Tuesday morning. Now, there's nothing wrong with Tuesday mornings. They a lot better than Monday mornings, but if you could choose, would you really want to spend every moment of every day for the next 6 weeks waiting for the weekend?

Neither would I.

Probably one of the only reasons for giving up booze for Lent, apart from religious observance, is to find out whether you drink too much. If you feel a lot better all the time (allowing for all the 'Tuesday-ness') then maybe you do drink too much. I didn't feel much different apart from Sunday mornings, for obvious reasons, and I didn't lose any weight either. This is because alcoholic drinks aren't very fattening. This may come as a surprise to some readers but it is true. You can argue that alcoholic drinks are fattening compared to lettuce but lettuce is no substitute for a gin and tonic (even a slimline gin and tonic with a slice of cucumber). The reality is that typical alcohol substitutes are all laden with calories and include:

- Horlicks
- Chocolate cake and coffee with real cream
- Ice cream

I found out why this is, by the way. It all goes back to our old friend 'self-control'. Apparently self-control depends on glucose levels in the brain and these levels drop later in the day. This explains why we tend to stray from the path of righteousness towards the evening. It's easy to resist a glass of rioja or a piece of chocolate at 10:30 on a Tuesday morning but a lot more difficult in the evening after a hard day, particularly if there are teenagers around.

So, give up booze for Lent if you must but don't expect miracles.

Reminisce About How Fab Everything Was When You Were Young

I know, I've said this before, but the 1970s weren't anything to write home about and they're not something I have fond memories of (with one or two exceptions). I suppose this is one of the consolations for someone of my generation. Although we are getting old and useless, everything around us is getting newer and more useful.

A colleague of mine bought his daughter along to a meeting we were attending (he was taking her back to 'Uni' for the start of the new term and it was on the way). So we got talking about when we were young and I mentioned how it was with no cellphones and social media and so on. She was quite perplexed and wanted to know how young people ever managed to socialize. I explained that we did have phones in our houses ('landlines' in modern parlance) and you would phone each other up and make plans to meet. The phones of course, were those old things with real bells in and came in a choice of three colours, black, cream or olive green (seriously!). You had to apply for one and wait 6 months for a man in a brown overall to come round and install it. It did mean that you often spent what seemed like an eternity waiting in the pub for your friends to arrive because the bus was cancelled or the train was late. I explained that in those days, many people didn't have bank accounts and were paid in cash every Friday afternoon (which is where the term 'pay-packet' comes from). The exact amount in notes and coins in a brown envelope. Housewives would queue up on Saturday mornings outside the offices of the gas company to pay their gas bills before their husbands had spent it all down the betting shop or at the pub.

Contrast this with the modern world. Hooray for the internet, electronic banking, E-Bay and all other modern conveniences and services that make life easier!

Adopt a Tree in the Sahara

It's a con. Trees don't grow in the Sahara.

Get a Part-Time Job in the Oxfam Shop

And get accused of being a pedophile or swamped with scones and strawberry jam.

Go to Art Classes

Unless the models are female and nude, then it's OK)

Take Lessons in any of the Following:

Pottery
Baking
Flower arranging
Creative writing

Day 12 The Wheels are Falling-Off

According to the experts at the Health and Safety Executive, everything starts to go pear-shaped after the age of fifty. Whereas in our younger days, we could pretend that we weren't feeling as good as we used to because we had too much to drink last night or had a cold, by the time you're past fifty, you start to run out of excuses and have to face up to the fact that you feel crap because you're old. There's no way around it, even if, like me, you didn't realise you were old, you are and that's all there is to it.

Just to cheer us all up, the experts have published a list of all the ways that we deteriorate when we get older, the buggeration factors of daily life that remind us that we are old.

How old is 'old'? The short answer to this question is, of course, that anyone older than you is 'old' and that anyone the same age as your children is 'young'. There is a large group of people in the middle who are neither old nor young. Thus, the concept of 'old age' depends on where you are starting from.

Ageing has to be distinguished from the passage of time. They are not the same. Although ageing depends on the passage of time, the body and the mind consist of an interconnected set of organs and processes. These processes can change at different rates in the same person, whereas the same organ or process can change at different rates in different people. In other words, bits of you age more quickly than others and older people, as a group, are more variable than younger people.

Ageing, then, is all about multiple subsystem failure. Successful ageing is all about trivial failures that can be easily compensated for. For most people, though, it is the subsystems that decline most quickly that are the most noticeable and make us realise that we are old.

Here are some examples:

Men: Erections

Women: Menopause

Both: Vision and hearing and the ability to recover from late nights and hangovers.

Day 11 More Depressing News About Age-related Decrements

Just to cheer us all up, here are more details of all the depressing things that happen to use as we get older.

Physical Capacity: The capacity of the body to deliver oxygen to the tissues is known as *aerobic capacity*. People with a high aerobic capacity are likely to be good at running marathons, cycling long distances or having sex for long periods of time without getting out of breath. The good news is that, when you get older, the temptation to run marathons or cycle long distances declines along with the ability to do it with any degree of competence. The bad news is that getting out of breath is the last thing you need to worry about when you are old and thinking about having sex.

Have you ever met those annoying people who like running? You might be in the pub or at a dinner party when one of the group mentions, casually, that they mustn't drink too much tonight because they've got to get up early tomorrow to go for a training run?

'I'm training for the London marathon', they say casually with a smug expression on their faces.

When you are young, it is difficult to know how to respond. Other people look at you as if to say,

'Have-you-ever-run-a-marathon-then-Bob-or-are-you going-to?'

Well, now that you are old, there's no need to feel embarrassed, you just turn to the trainee runner, smile sympathetically and say,

'Rather you than me. I tried it when I was young, too old now. I'm going to have a long lie-in tomorrow. Pass the Port, please.'

Although the temptation to run for long periods declines quickly with age, the desire to have sex for long periods does not. Unfortunately, this is one of those desires that seems to decline at a slower rate than one's aerobic capacity, resulting in a mismatches between one's aims and objectives and the resources available to achieve them. This is a mismatch that can lead to some difficult and embarrassing moments. The real danger, of course, is that miserable old bastards like us will just keel over with a heart attack half-way through. A nice way to go, you might think, but if a job's worth doing it's worth doing properly and that means finishing it and tidying up afterwards, which is difficult to do if you're being carted-off to the emergency ward in an ambulance.

Less spectacular, but if anything, even more irksome, is the prospect of what we might term 'hydraulic collapse' due to overexertion. Basically, what happens is that after bonking merrily away for a while, our cardio-vascular system can longer meet the competing demands of supplying blood to the muscles to bonk, to the skin, to dissipate the heat created as a result of all the excitement and for the hydraulic requirements to 'keep the flag flying' so to speak.

Young blokes worry about premature ejaculation.

When you're old, you should be so lucky. Stop moaning, just be grateful if you can still bring things to a satisfying conclusion without running out of breath or having a heart attack.

Here are some other fab things that make ageing so enjoyable:

- Your general health may decline and your blood pressure may increase, particularly if you gain weight. No more salty pork scratchings washed down with Irish Cream liquor then.
- Your grip strength may decline, making it more likely that you will drop an icy can of refreshing lager onto the new carpet in the living room.
- Your lifting strength will decline – making it more difficult to lower that case of fine wines from the top shelf of the cupboard.
- Your balance will decline increasing the risk of falling, particularly if you have just sampled the wine (above). This is why old people's homes don't have balconies.
- Your eyesight will decline making it more difficult to read the fine print on a bottle of red wine (you buy the 11% alcohol special offer thinking it is 14.5% and only realise your mistake next morning because you feel fine).
- Your hearing will decline and you may miss the call for 'last orders' at the pub.
- Your reaction time will slow and you may fail to catch a bottle of wine that your partner knocks off the table by accident.
- Your limb motility will slow, making the above even more likely.
- Your tissue elasticity/joint mobility will decrease making it difficult to bend and reach for the bottle of export strength gin at the back of the supermarket shelf.
- Your tolerance for paced work will decline and you will become increasingly intolerant about being nagged that you didn't tidy the garage yesterday because you drank too much the night before.
- Your ability to recover from slips and trips will decline making it more likely that you will fall down the stairs after a heavy night on the way to the bathroom in yet another attempt to empty your bladder.

Day 10: How to Spot Old People

Today, I decided that I was going to prepare for old age by having a 'spot the old person' competition with myself.

You could argue that this is utterly vain as well as being pointless because you can't hide your age even if you understand all the cues. Anyway, here's a handy list of cues to help you identify old people. These cues are useful because they even work if you've forgotten your glasses.

One of easiest ways to spot an old person is by watching what happens when they try to run. It's hilarious! A pair of knees lasts about fifty years and it's all downhill after that. Same with hips, they last a bit longer but lose flexibility. The older runner lacks stride length and knee flexion and the result is a flat-footed kind of running of foreshortened steps. As the aged runner totters along with a mincing gait, his upper body seems in constant danger of jack-knifing forward over his legs.

In many ways, old people are their own worst enemies, or their knees' worst enemies. Why is it that perfectly sane, healthy people turn into decrepit morons the minute they retire? They sell the family home in a nice suburb like Purley or Morden and buy a bungalow by the sea-side. There is an enormous strip of land along the south coast of England from Eastbourne in the East to Bournemouth in the West - the bungalow belt. It's full of old people who can't walk properly anymore because they've got "bungalow knees" weakened by years of not having to climb the stairs. They're everywhere, clogging-up the pavements of otherwise delightful English seaside towns, tottering along on their way to the Tea Rooms or to the Library or to the chemist to buy some laxatives. These are the people who get in your way when you're on an emergency visit to the off-licence.

After a few more years of not climbing the stairs, nature takes its course and after a while, they can't walk at all. Then, they buy one of those mobility scooters and clutter-up the High Street of old English towns. Personally, I think that these things are a menace and should be banned. One of the funniest things I read in the paper recently was a story about an old person on a mobility scooter who was returning from the pub one night and lost control of his scooter. It veered down a grassy bank and fell into the municipal boating lake. The lake was only three feet deep, but when the "emergency rescue services" arrived they refused to walk-in and rescue the poor bastard on the grounds that they hadn't received the right health and safety training for dealing with aquatic rescues. The poor bastard died of course.

You couldn't make it up, really you couldn't. Someone should have told the rescue service personnel that one day, they too, will be old and the older you get, the more likely it is that you will find yourself in the shit and will need to be rescued.

Day 9 What to do with an Ageing Population

The problem with ageing is that there is no excuse for it. Old people have been around for too long and that's all there is to it. No excuses, no complaints, no, "Err but I've lived a good and honest life" The definition of old age is someone of advanced years, i.e. too many of them for his or her own good. You can't sit on the fence - if you're old, you're old and that's all there is to it.

One of the most interesting things about ageing is that we don't know that it is happening to us until it is too late.

How many times do we meet people who can't walk up the stairs without stopping to rest, who wear clothes that three other people could get into and who are always ill and never happy?

Are these people old? No, they are people who are being run over by a train in slow motion. They just didn't see it coming until it was too late. And that says a lot because if you can't get out of the way of a train that is hurtling down on you at a speed of three miles per year, what hope do you have?

Now, I think that it is a mistake to confuse obesity with age, or fatness with age, or even diseases with age. In the modern world, most infectious diseases and many other problems can be dealt with fairly easily. The modern dilemma is that now, we have a large number of old people who are not fat, not sick, not unhealthy, quite happy and totally oblivious to the fact that everybody else thinks they are old.

It's not their fault they were born a long time ago. Or is it? What are we going to do with them? Well, I suppose we could put them into service in Victorian WALLED GARDENS and give them Hessian bags full of cow shit to soak in rainwater while playing the teletubbies 'MAN IN THE HOUSE' sketch to them in the background. We could feed them with 1970's dog food and make chalk sculptures out of their turds to beat Tracy Emin and all the Britpop artists to the next Turner prize.

Day 8 Memory Deficits

We went to a fancy dress party at the tennis club the other day. A mate of mine came as Serena Williams and my wife came as Gloria Esteban. I couldn't be bothered with all that nonsense, dressing up in silly clothes and feeling like a complete idiot while pretending to enjoy yourself.

So I went as the Doppler Effect with a blue light on my chest and a red light on my back.

It was easy to do. Whenever anyone asked me what I had come dressed as, I told them the truth, adding that I was going to come dressed as a 'deja-vu' experience but I'd had a funny feeling I'd done that before.

If they persisted, I just said,

"I'm sure I just told you? I've got a funny feeling we've had this conversation before…"

Is it possible for someone with Alzheimer's disease to have a deja-vu experience? I've been puzzling about this for quite some time.

I would have thought that you can only have a deja-experience if a newly experienced event triggers a faint memory of something similar, so you get the feeling that you have experienced it before.

So, if you have Alzheimer's disease, there must be something in memory that the new experience triggers in order to give rise to the deja-vu experience and if you had Alzheimer's disease, there wouldn't be.

Is this true though? Maybe people with Alzheimer's disease only have faint memories of the few things that they do remember. In which case, they'd be having deja-vu experiences all the time and be living in a perpetual 'ground-hog day' scenario until all the memories are gone and they die.

One things for sure, they wouldn't be able to have a deja-vu experience of being dead, would they?

Plenty to look forward to then…..unless it's already happened.

Old age has a way of creeping up on you, when you least expect it. I arrived home from work the other day, feeling surprisingly chirpy (for a man of my age). So, I decided that a trip to the gym to do some exercise was in order. I made myself a cup of tea, trotted up the stairs to the bedroom and got changed into my shorts and gym top. When I finished my tea, I put my car keys in one pocket and the house key and my cellphone in the other. I bounded downstairs, checking in the kitchen that there was food out on the table for dinner, and then I headed for the gym. When I got back from the gym, I couldn't find my phone. I looked in the car. It wasn't there and so I went back to the gym and asked the receptionist if anyone had handed-in a phone. She looked at me sympathetically and shook her head.

'Oh dear', I said.

Have you ever had that feeling of elation when you discover that you didn't lose your car keys/wallet, passport after all? I was trying to remember what that feeling was like as I crawled on my hands and knees looking for my phone under the gym machines. I went back to receptionist and asked her to phone me if anyone handed-in a phone. She said she would and nodded with the kind of expression on her face that said,

'You've lost your phone, you silly old sod, no-one is going to hand it in even if they do find it because you obviously didn't lose it here because someone would have handed it in already if you had.'

So, I went back home, trying to retrace my steps mentally, in search of clues about where to look next. When I got home, I had a brainwave and asked my wife to phone me. If the phone was in the house, I would hear it ringing and would soon find it. My wife gave me the kind of look that suggested that it was about time I lost my phone because, like me, it was out of date, too old and in need of replacement. Anyway, she phoned me but it didn't work - we heard nothing. I went upstairs to our bedroom and I heard nothing. I went down to the kitchen and heard nothing. Eventually, I decided to stop searching and went to the kitchen to cook dinner instead, hoping that if I stopped thinking about the phone, I might have one of those experiences when memories bubble-up to the rescue when you least expect them.

One of the ingredients in that night's recipe came in a packet with some instructions written in small pink letters against a beige background. This is the kind of labelling that challenges people of my age. So, I went to the cupboard under the stairs to get my reading glasses, which were in my briefcase. When I get home from work, I always put my briefcase in the same place on a shelf in the cupboard under the stairs. I have many sets of reading glasses, all the same, which I keep in different parts of the house for reading illegible instructions on challenging consumer products. If in doubt, my briefcase is the first place I look when I need my reading glasses

I reached into the briefcase in the dark and felt something familiar. That 'I haven't lost my wallet after all!' feeling hit me as my phone slipped into my hand in a familiar way. There is a pleasant kind of denial that is both reassuring and worrying when you realise that have been behaving perfectly normally (for you) without realising it. All was well and there was never anything to worry about, except that I had forgotten that I was old and began to wonder who the other person was who couldn't find the phone the he never even lost in the first place. I went to tell my wife who asked me why I hadn't been able to find my phone when it was in my briefcase all the time. I couldn't answer her question.

Then it came to me.

It was all to do with 'goal-switching'.

The main goal was to go to the gym. Putting the phone in the pocket of my gym trousers (three quarter length Adidas gym trousers, left hand pocket) is part of that goal. On the way out, I had gone to the kitchen to check on the food and momentarily switched to cooking the dinner mode without realising it. A subgoal of the cooking the dinner goal is to put the phone away in my briefcase, so that I won't put it down somewhere and lose it.

Isn't it ironic that it's the important stuff that gets lost when memory lapses. The lapses themselves are unforgettable!

So, summing it all up from the perspective of memory, here is an example of memory in action:

A man and his wife go for a drive to the county of Gloucestershire, because they have never visited Gloucestershire before (or if they have, they've both forgotten). They decide to have lunch at a nice country pub. Sitting in the pub, the man has a deja-vu experience – he has the feeling that he has visited the pub before. However, he knows that his memory isn't as good as it used to be. So, he leans over to his wife and asks:

"Darling, have you ever had a deja-vu experience?"

To which she replies:

"Why do you keep asking me that?"

Given that there are only two people having this conversation, how would either of them know whether the other one has Alzheimer's disease or not?

Day 7 More Horrors About Ageing.

According to my friends at the Health and Saferty Executive (remember the HSE with all its fat, unhealthy staff laughing at us because we're old) older people have lowered tolerance for heat and cold.

I hate to say it, but I think they are right, so last Christmas when I was walking around the supermarket I bought myself a Father Christmas 'onesie' (one piece pyjama suit with a hood and a zip to close it at the front.

Shakespeare would be proud of me. These are adult versions of the pyjama suits we wear on young children and toddlers. They are soft and very warm.

One of the more positive aspects of ageing is that you get better at DIY, but only when you have to be. Modern cars are a complete mystery to me. Gone are the days when you could remove the cylinder head of a family car and recondition it, maybe regrind the valves and put some new gaskets in to make it work better. Nowadays you need special tools and a computer if you're lucky enough to even find it in the first place.

Dishwashers are a different story though. It was during the noughties that the battle of the dishwasher finally came to end in the Bridger residence, but only after a 4:0 victory by me against my wife. We bought the dishwasher in 1999 when we moved into the house and by about 2008, it had started to switch itself off and end its cycle prematurely, leaving puddles of water in the bottom. My wife, of course, demanded that we buy a new one immediately. But I was not going to surrender so easily. So, on a Saturday morning with a handful of tools and some scruffy clothes I went into battle. After removing a few screws and and the inside cover, I noticed that some wires were looking rather corroded and loose. So I disconnected them and cleaned them with emery cloth until they were shiny. Then I reconnected them and put everything back together. Filling the dishwasher with the contents of the sink, which, by now, was overflowing, I switched it on and closed the door.

Nothing happened.

So I opened the door, switched it off, unplugged at the wall and then reconnected everything again.

It worked. It worked again three more times before the dishwasher finally died of old age. My wife was delighted of course and we bought a brand new dishwasher the very next day.

We just goes to show that even though death is inevitable, you should never give up without a fight.

Day 6 Self Awareness is Vital

Even I am not so vain as to believe, even for a second, that when a gorgeous 22-year-old postgraduate student looks at me in the middle of a lecture with a naughty smile on her face, that she is attracted to me.

Let's get one thing straight. Gorgeous 22-year-old females are not attracted to old men like me. This seems obvious to most people, but it is something you have to remind yourself of constantly when you don't realise you are old.

I'd been giving a lecture on the biomechanics of the human spine and how the different postures that we adopt in daily life can load our backs in different ways. From this, it is easy to understand why certain postures and movements cause back pain in some people. Old people are prone to some kinds of back pain, of course, but one of the few blessings of age is that back pain becomes less severe or even disappears completely. In young people, the spine is like a three-dimensional jigsaw puzzle. As long as all the pieces fit together properly, all is well. However, there are many different pieces, some are made of bone, some of cartilage and there are muscles and tendons and nerves and blood vessels. It's all very complicated and sudden knocks and strains can create 'hot spots'of pressure and loading that cause pain. In old backs, the soft bits, like the discs, start to shrink and other bits ossify and the spine loses flexibility. The result is that they lose flexibility and are therefore less likely to get into trouble.

During the lecture, I had explained the evolution of the upright posture in humans, the anatomical differences between humans and chimpanzees and why humans can stand upright with ease and grace, whereas chimpanzees stand clumsily and with effort.

As I explained all this, I demonstrated the difference in postures myself, by adopting them. A highlight of this lecture, one that keeps the students awake and generates enthusiasm and interest, is when I explain in words and movements the structural differences between the ape pelvis and the human pelvis and then show the functional consequences of these differences. I climbed onto the table at the front of the lecture theatre, adopted a quadrupedal position and then mimicked a chimpanzee trying to stand up. The students found this hilarious, as they always do. Next, I jumped off the table and did my impersonation of a chimpanzee trying to walk on two legs. More laughter.

Having made the point, I resumed the lecture and showed some equations that can be used to calculate the forces acting on the spine in different positions of the body. It was then that I noticed that a very pretty young girl, sitting at the back of the room, was smiling at me. She was blond, about 22, well dressed, with a little make-up –the kind of girl who attracts attention from men of all ages, in fact and in largely the same way.

For a moment, a very brief one I must admit, I wondered whether she might be interested in me. Clearly, that was extremely unlikely and there had to be a better explanation. I carried on talking and looked at the faces of the other students in the audience. They all seemed normal, attentive and interested in my lecture. Then I looked again at the girl at the back. She was still smiling at me. The smile was a little disconcerting, friendly, yes, naughty, a little, amused, certainly. It was a subtle smile, the kind of smile that someone makes when something is wrong. I wasn't sure whether she was smiling with me or at me, but there was also a suggestion pity. Something was definitely wrong.

Images of schoolboy days came into my mind, of snotty-faced little schoolboys who've forgotten their handkerchiefs. I checked my nose, nope, no evidence of snot. I looked back at the girl. She didn't seem to be looking at me directly in the eye, her gaze was cast downwards slightly. I shuffled behind the lectern, and without taking my eyes off the audience, I checked down below.

My fly had come undone.

It's at times like these that a cool head and a steady hand are useful. Trying to pretend that I hadn't noticed, I carried on talking and sat down behind the lecture table. Slowly, I did my fly up, while looking at the audience to keep their attention on my face. Well, I think I got away with it. As I continued the lecture, I looked at the girl at the back and, sure enough, she had stopped smiling.

She just looked at me in a knowing way. There are many secrets that I would like to share with a beautiful 22 year-old girl.

This isn't one of them.

Anyway, lesson learned – when a young woman smiles at you, you know you've done or said something stupid.

Day 5: Age Related Improvements

With only a few days to go before the beginning of the end, I am coming to the conclusion that getting old isn't as bad as it is made out and that there are, in fact a number of advantages.

It is undeniably true that older people have better coping skills than the young. This is because they have had a lot more practice and are better at handling disappointment. I remember when my wife told me that there would be no food at our tennis club New Year's Eve party, I took it in the chin. Sometimes you just have to take your medicine like a grown-up and not complain. In the case of our tennis club, of course, most of the complaints are about the food, not the absence of it and so it would seem that we are all going to have a fabulous time on December 31. The lady who manages our bar and catering facilities has something of the 1970s about her. I remember in the 1970s, commuters were referred to scathingly, by the British Rail staff as 'passengers' and told that the train was delayed because there were leaves on the railway line (they were lied to in other words, the lazy bastards were on strike again). The Post Office Telephone Department would tell you that you couldn't have a second telephone installed in your house because you already had one and shouldn't be so selfish. I went to a restaurant once with a girlfriend and we both got food poisoning after eating the partridge. When I complained, the manager, instead of giving me a refund or a bottle of wine or two, gave me a voucher for a free dinner for two (knowing full well that we wouldn't risk it).
> In the case of Denise, our bar and catering manageress, I can offer a number of observations. Firstly, she knows nothing about food or drink and ignores requests for more variety and a wider selection of food and drink. She also ignores customer demands. If a beer is popular with the members she stops ordering it because she has to keep changing the barrel. She offers food that nobody ever buys (pies, for example). She is good at making chips though and she does sell a lot of them. But, like Party Sevens and Martini at late night parties in the 1970s, you shouldn't assume that demand for a product or service reflects quality without considering the supply side.

People will put up with anything if that's all there is.

I think older people have a lower prevalence of stress at work than the young. There are a number of sound reasons for this, of course. One is that they have had more practice at ducking before the solids hit the fan. Another one is that, whereas the young are motivated by ambition and the need to get on in life, do well and be admired by their peers, older workers couldn't give a shit about any of this. Let's face it, people only get stressed about work if they actually care about their jobs.

Older people definitely have better anticipation. Well the surviving ones do anyway. When you are old, you can't get out of the way as quickly or react as fast, so anticipation is vital if you are to get out of the way before the shit hits the fan. The same applies to alcohol, of course. Whereas youngsters are always keen to experiment with cocktails and other concoctions, anyone over 45 years of age knows to go nowhere near the large bowl of punch at the drinks reception. It may taste like Ribena and look healthy with bits of fruit floating in it, but we know better. Be boring, stick to gin and tonic or sherry and you'll make it through the night.

I think older people also have better social skills. Having an improved repertoire of responses enables them to insult other people more politely and not feel rude when we decline a glass of gluwhein at the office Christmas party. I was at a reception the other day and in conversation with one of the 'Metropolitan Elite' (at least, that's how the tabloid newspapers refer to them). She lived in a large house in North London, worked in University Administration and was married to a journalist. Her two children went to the best state schools London has to offer. She was complaining about the government refusing to take more Syrian refugees, of it being uncaring about the needs of transgender teenagers and generally, of not giving enough taxpayers' money away to causes that she believed in. After listening politely and saying nothing, I waited for her to ask me what I thought. I sipped on my sherry and replied that I had no opinions at all about any of these matters, knew nothing about student politics and didn't care about social issues.

Well, that's one way of getting rid of annoying people without telling them to 'fuck-off'.

I think old people have better strategic focus. You finally understand that you don't need to worry about the future because you haven't got one. In healthy ageing, the vanity of youth is sacrificed on the altar of expediency as we learn to relax, let go, have a drink.....nothing to worry about.

Day 4 Enjoying the Ironies of a Life Well-Lived

One of the advantages of age is that one develops a better insight into oneself and can begin to enjoy the ironies of a life lived-well. For example, I once wrote a book about giving up booze for Lent. It sold quite well and so I spent the royalties on booze.

One of the advantages of having an obsessive compulsive personality is that you're never bored – there always something to do….

….or something to do again because you got it wrong the first time….

…or something to do again, just to be on the safe side…

…or something to do again because you can't remember whether you've already done it….

…. or something to do again because you think you remember that you've already done it but you don't trust your memory…

…or something to do because there's no harm in double checking, is there?

So, never a dull moment for those with OCD tendencies.

Obsessive tendencies don't apply to everything, of course. Alcohol is a good example. There's always been a kind of circadian ambivalence in my attitudes towards alcohol. My attitudes towards it seem to vary according to a 24-hour cycle. In the mornings when I wake-up, I can't stand the stuff and never want to drink a single drop again.

In the evenings on the other hand, there is nothing more appealing than a foaming glass of hoppy Indian Pale Ale except, perhaps a 250ml goblet full of ruby red Rioja.

When I gave up booze for Lent a few years ago, the main effect was a complete disruption to my normal 24-hour rhythm. When I woke up in the morning, I felt great and had no attitudes towards alcohol at all. That, in itself, was a revelation. When you've had strong views about something for over 40 years and these views vary wildly over the day, it is extremely odd not to have any views about it at all. In the evenings, I found myself doing things that I would normally do earlier in the day (like drinking tea) and walking around supermarkets looking for special offers. In fact, the world becomes quite surreal when one is sober all the time. It feels like Tuesday morning all the time.
I suppose some of you might be wondering whether, in the absence of any thoughts about alcohol I might have developed my views about other topics, perhaps topics of a more adult and socially meaningful nature.

Hardly, I've never been interested in student politics or social issues of any kind and I'm completely lacking in empathy.

Sex on the other hand is different. This in one of those things that I'm always interested in and positively disposed towards, regardless of my internal state. The capability to actually engage in it varies in an increasingly embarrassing and inconvenient way as one ages and even obsessive compulsive personality traits aren't much help.

I did wonder whether giving up booze for Lent would have an impact in the bedroom. Interestingly, it had no effect whatsoever on the capability to engage in it but there was an effect on 'deployability'. I'm not sure my wife appreciated this though.

Socrates said that an unexamined life is not worth living. Somebody else said drink deeply from the cup of life for tomorrow we die.
I say,

Day 3: Getting a Grip on Retirement Planning

Retirement planning is something to get serious about when you are old. A friend of mine told me a story about what happened to him when he retired.

There are important lessons to be learned here.

The Main Characters

Alaistair Dunglenning (my friend): Retired lecturer in double entry book-keeping who rented out his flat in Cheamsford and retired to a mobile home in Hove.

Kevin Betts: School friend of Alaistair and lapsed mycologist who became an investment banker. Loves money but hates banking in particular and people in general.

Damien Greene: Friend of Kevin's who met a nymphomiac landlady in 1979 and has lived with her in the pub ever since. Has a red face, purple nose and likes to dye his hair blond in the summer.

Janice: Long-suffering girlfriend of Alaister, a beautiful angel and far too good for him in the first place.

Background

In order to supplement his pension, Alaistair has rented his flat out to a charitable organization at a rate of 500 GBP per month – a third of the going rate When Kevin finds out, he is furious and is determined to get Alastair a better deal. Damien has nothing else to do, so he comes along as well.

Here's what happened:

Act 1 *Coming for the Rent*

It was a peaceful Sunday morning deep in the heart of Sussex. Alaistair was tucked up warmly in bed. He was lying on his side next to Janice, who had her back to him. His lower body was wedged, snugly, against the soft curves of her shapely buttocks. His face nestled in her mousy brown hair. Her perfume filled his nose and his left hand was resting on something that he had once mistaken for the hot water bottle his Aunt Margaret had bought him for his 21st birthday. He was floating in a sea of warm and soft sensations, happily and pleasantly lost in the "no-man's land" somewhere between being asleep and being awake.

Suddenly, the telephone rang.

Alaistair rolled reluctantly away from the sleeping Janice and picked-up the phone. Unfortunately for him, Kevin was at the other end of it and was screaming at him.

'Ugh!' he groaned as what felt like paint stripper being squirted into the side of his head.

'Who's speaking?' he demanded, gingerly replacing the receiver to his ear.

'It's me, Kevin,' replied Kevin.

Alaistair looked at his watch. It was 7:00 AM. 'Why are you phoning me so early, Kev? It's my day-off. It's Sunday (being recently retired, every day was Alaister's day off, but he hadn't quite got the hang of it yet).

Kevin explained to Alaistair that the night before, he and Damien had paid a visit to Alaistair's flat, fulfilling their promise to check on the identity of Alaistair's mysterious tenants:

"The Afro-Euro-Asiatic Women's Street Collective Amalgam".

Act 2 *A Surprise Visit*

They had arrived at the flat after eleven o'clock at night, aiming for the element of surprise. At first, the situation hadn't looked very promising. An ugly woman in scruffy clothes had answered the door and looked at them in an unfriendly way. Damien and Kevin had introduced themselves and explained that they were representatives of the landlord and had come round to check on the flat and to find out whether the tenants were having any problems. Kevin had become suspicious when the woman replied brusquely that there were no problems at all, that everything was fine and had then tried to close the door in their faces. When they had tried to stall her, she resisted and while this was happening they overheard muffled, giggling noises coming from inside the flat. As the woman started to shut the door again, Damien had asked whether he could use the bathroom.

Reluctantly, the ugly woman had let them in. But before she did, she said that she had to warn her "sisters" that some *men* were coming into the flat. She shut the door quickly. Damien and Kevin listened carefully and heard more giggling noises followed by hasty, rustling sounds and doors closing. Something which sounded as if it had springs in it made a squeaking noise, groaned and then clunked. Damien and Kevin had become even more suspicious when they heard this and waited, impatiently, for the door to open.

After a few moments, the ugly woman returned and let them in. As soon as they walked through the doorway, she started spraying them with insecticide. Then, she climbed up onto a coffee table and sprayed all around the living room. 'We're very careful about hygiene around here,' she explained, helpfully.

The flat looked more or less as they remembered it when Alaistair had lived there – except that there was a pile of mattresses stacked in the corner of the living room with sheets folded on top. Kevin looked around and walked over to the pile of mattresses.

'They're for when we do charity collections,' said the ugly woman hastily. 'The sisters stay here overnight on Fridays and then go to the shops to do their collections on Saturday.'

Damien had disappeared to investigate the bathroom, from where he managed to emit some suitably convincing noises to disguise his real intentions.

'So how many of you are there living here?' asked Kevin. 'In a flat this size, the maximum number of tenants is three.'

The ugly woman looked at him defensively. 'Well, yes, there's only two of us living here full-time but we do have others round to stay sometimes, as I said, err, for street collections and the like.'

'I see,' said Kevin sniffing the air carefully. Something was wrong. Very wrong. The name of the supposed charitable organisation that was renting Alaistair's flat was highly suggestive of particular things. Certainly, the name was entirely consistent with the appearance and manner of the ugly woman. There she stood with an aerosol of CFC-free insecticide in her hand, squinting at him through John Lennon spectacles. She had short brown hair the colour of well-rotted manure, no make-up, corduroy trousers, a baggy orange pullover and hiking boots. But Kevin was certain that he could smell something else, something that had been there before the ugly woman had started spraying. It smelled suspiciously like a combination of stale booze, perfume, make-up and all the other paraphernalia associated with feminine hygiene. He looked around the flat. On the coffee table next to the insecticide spray, was a cell-phone.

'Something's wrong,' thought Kevin. But he couldn't identify what it was. Just then, Damien appeared from the bathroom with both hands stuffed into his pockets. With his back to the ugly woman, he winked at Kevin.

'OK, Kevin, let's go, everything's fine by the look of it,' he said quickly. Kevin nodded and they walked through the doorway faster than a couple of journalists going into a pub at opening time. They clambered down the creaking stairs, edging past Colin the Cat who belonged to the Portugese window cleaner who lived downstairs and was doing something revolting to his nether regions. They looked away and walked briskly across the road to Kevin's car.

'Something's up,' said Kevin as they got into the car.

'You're telling me!' said Damien, 'look what I found in the bog.' Damien emptied his pockets and out came hundreds of cotton wool balls of different pastel shades. Some of them were damp with traces of liquids of various kinds, others were smeared with make-up, bright red lipstick, dark eye shadow and sooty blobs of mascara. 'The rubbish bin was empty. Found 'em stuffed under a towel in the cupboard under the sink.'

Kevin was impressed – not only that Damien had managed to uncover some important clues about the true nature of the Afro-Euro-Asiatic Women's Street Collective Amalgam, but that he had managed to do it while making a creatively impressive range of noises suggestive of a quite different set of activities. They sat quietly for a moment, trying to assess the significance of their findings in relation to the supposed charitable activities of the collective.

'They couldn't be Janice's, could they? Left over from when she and Alaistair were staying here?' asked Kevin.

'No chance, mate. For a start, there's too many of them,' replied Damien, expertly sniffing the colourful little cloudlets of cotton wool. 'Besides, most of these are pretty fresh.'

They decided to stake out the flat and wait to see if anything suspicious happened. By this time, the pubs were closed so there wasn't much else to do until the following morning. They looked up at the bedroom and living room windows. The lights were on. After about 20 minutes, the bedroom light went off. The silhouettes of two people appeared in the living room. They were soon joined by a third. One went back into the bedroom while the taller of the two figures in the living room handed something to the other and then walked towards the front door.

'Get down!' said Kevin, 'Someone's coming.'

Damien and Kevin slid their buttocks forwards in their seats, submarining until they could just see out of the window, 'Up periscope,' Damien thought to himself. The front door opened and a distinguished looking man in a sports jacket and twill trousers appeared. He was smoking a cigarette. He flipped a cloth cap onto his head, pulling it down over his forehead and walked quickly over to a Jaguar car. In a moment, he was gone.

'What do you make of that?' asked Damien.

Kevin scratched the side of his head. 'Posh bloke in a jag visiting a "wimmin's" charity late at night. Maybe he went to make a donation?'

'Maybe,' agreed Damien, 'but what kind of donation?' he wondered.

'Right,' said Kevin, after a few minutes 'Let's think this through. Alaistair rents his flat to a crowd that call themselves the Afro-Euro-Asiatic Women's Street Collective Amalgam. They tell him they're a charity, so he lets them have it for a few quid a week. We come round and this ugly woman in horrible clothes answers the door and doesn't want to let us in. Then we hear some funny noises. When we finally manage to talk our way in, she's spraying the room and us with insecticide. Then you find all those cotton wool balls in the bathroom. The living room's full of spare mattresses and sheets and the place smells of booze, make-up and insecticide. What do you reckon?'

'Things are not what they seem, that's what I reckon,' replied Damien.

'Not at all what they seem,' agreed Kevin.

They decided to wait a little longer in case anything else happened. After about 10 minutes, a large black Mercedes appeared and parked outside the flat. A man with dark glasses, black trousers, a black pullover and a black jacket got out of the car and walked quickly to the front door. He rang the bell and in no time at all, a woman answered. She was not the same woman that Kevin and Damien had spoken to earlier, but she *was* ugly and she *was* wearing scruffy clothes. They exchanged a few words very briefly, and she let him in.

'Now what?' said Damien.

'I'm going to have a look!' said Kevin. He got out of the car and closed the door as softly as he could. Stooping slightly, he tip-toed across the road to the Mercedes. Peering through the window he saw a business card on the dashboard. There was a picture of a scantily clad blonde next the words:

Sexy Stacy, The Old Vicarage, Beddingham Close, Upper Whallup, The Cotswolds.

Next he crept across to the front of Alaistair's flat. With his back to the wall and his hands spread-eagled against it, Kevin looked from side to side and edged towards the front door. He knelt down and pushed the letterbox open. Putting his ear to the opened box, he listened intently.

Kevin turned and signaled to Damien to join him at the door.

'More funny noises!' hissed Kevin as Damien crouched next to him. They strained their ears but couldn't tell what was happening in the flat. 'We'll have to look inside,' said Kevin, 'but how do we get up to the first floor?'

'Hang-on,' whispered Damien, 'The bloke who lives downstairs, y'know, Colin the Cat's old man. He's a window cleaner isn't he?'

'Dunno,' replied Kevin.

'I think he is,' said Damien, 'and I think he keeps his ladders round the back.'

Damien crept softly round to the back of the building. The window cleaner's van was parked next to some rubbish bins. He looked in the back window of the van.

'Jackpot!' thought Damien as he squinted in the poor light. 'It's a LADA van. LADA owners never bother to lock their cars because they know that nobody would ever be stupid enough to steal a LADA.' Sure enough, the back doors of the van were unlocked. Damien opened them and found a telescopic ladder inside. He lifted the ladder out of the back of the van and stealthily carried it round to the front of the house.

'Brilliant!' said Kevin as Damien rounded the corner with ladder over his shoulder. They extended the ladder and placed it carefully next to the drainpipe by the bedroom window. A nasty surprise was waiting for Kevin at the top of the ladder. He climbed up quickly, and, leaning across towards the window, peered through a gap in the lace curtains. Then he saw it. The ugly woman was sitting on the edge of the bed removing her hiking boots. The man in black sat in a leather armchair opposite her. He had a drink in one hand and a cigarette in the other. Kevin grimaced at as she started to pull-off her thick woollen socks. He held his breath as she peeled-off a thick, grey, knee-length woollen sock. To his utter surprise, it revealed a petite white foot with bright red painted toenails the shape of dragon's teeth. Another sock was soon lying on the floor next to the first one, and was quickly followed by the baggy corduroy trousers which, when removed, revealed a pair of exquisitely shaped legs.

'Bloody hell!' thought Kevin.

'What's going on!' demanded Damien.

'Wait!' hissed Kevin.

He looked back into the bedroom just in time to see the ugly woman disappear behind a screen, with a flash of red satin underwear. She emerged a few minutes later wearing make-up, a long blond wig and very little else. She walked towards the man in black with an undulating gait, the voluptuous curves of her gorgeous body moved sensuously as she approached him. She cocked her head to one side, put both hands behind her neck and pushed her hair so that it tumbled suggestively over the front of her shoulders. Then she looked at him with a devastatingly sexy expression.

'You're early tonight, Frank,' she said invitingly. She tilted the John Lennon glasses up onto her forehead and winked at him. An explosion of raw sexuality hit Kevin directly in the groin and he nearly fell-off the ladder.

'You know I always like to be first,' replied the man in black, fanning himself with a wad of ten pound notes.

'So that's what they're up to,' thought Kevin. 'It's all a front!' He climbed down the ladder and started to explain to Damien. Damien listened in astonishment as Kevin described the scene upstairs.

'Never! No! come off it,' he hissed as Kevin whispered to him, explaining that the ugly woman wasn't ugly at all and was, in fact, the best looking prostitute he had ever seen, not that he'd seen many, honest, and that at that very moment she was upstairs with a client.

'Incredible, who would have thought!' exclaimed Damien, 'my turn to have a look!'

Damien climbed, unsteadily, up the ladder and peered through the crack in the curtains. He looked down at Kevin and pursed his lips, putting his right wrist into the crook of his left elbow and waiving his left fist around in the air.

'Get down!' hissed Kevin, 'we've got to get out of here.' Gesticulating wildly, Damien suddenly lost his balance. With his arms flailing the air and his hips gyrating, his upper body toppled away from the ladder. The last thing that Damien saw before he hit the ground was his left foot saying goodbye to the second rung from the top of the ladder. After that, everything went black. The next thing he became aware of was his head sliding along the pavement towards the kerb. He opened his eyes just in time to see his feet sticking up in the air, one on each side of Kevin, who was pulling him back towards the car. Soon afterwards, his head arrived at the edge of the pavement and hit the gutter with a sound like a pumpkin falling off a kitchen table onto a cold stone floor. Everything went black again.

Act 3 *We've Come for the Rent*

Kevin opened the door of the car and manhandled Damien onto the back seat. 'Quick,' he said, 'Let's go.' The bedroom curtains parted as the beautiful blond looked-out to find out what all the noise was about. The first thing she saw was the ladder. As she looked up, Kevin's car rounded the corner, just in time to elude her. Kevin parked the car a few streets away and turned to check on Damien. Fortunately, Damien was coming round. He had found a generous supply of miniature whiskey bottles, which Kevin had stolen from the drinks trolley during his last business class flight.

'Bloody good disguise, eh?' gasped Kevin. 'I'd never have thought she was a pro, not in a million years!'

'I was convinced she was a disabled, lesbian, one parent minority family,' said Damien rubbing the back of his head. 'The Afro-Euro-Asiatic

Women's Street Collective Amalgam! What a brilliant name for a brothel! What a wonderful disguise! What camouflage! What imagination! What a fantastic front!'

'More front than a front door!' agreed Kevin, in admiration. He slapped the steering wheel of his car with both hands. 'Anyway, back to business. Now, what are we going to do?'

'Tell Alaistair and get him some more rent, of course,' replied Damien. 'And I think we'd better go back to the flat *now*. The element of surprise is on our side. We can arrive suddenly, catch them unawares and say that the man downstairs has complained to us about the noise coming from the flat. As the landlord's representatives we demand to know what's going on.'

'Let's go then!' agreed Kevin.

Act 4 *Negotiations*

Kevin drove quickly back to the flat and parked the car outside the bedroom window. He revved the engine loudly as he switched off the ignition. The engine stopped with a loud stutter. They both got out of the car, slamming the doors as loudly as they could and walked briskly up to the front door.

'Open-up. We know you're awake!' demanded Kevin, banging his fist rudely on the glass windowpane of the front door.

'And we know what you're up to!' shouted Damien. The neighbours have just phoned us about you. We've got a list of complaints as long as your arm. Let us in!'

They heard footsteps as somebody came downstairs to the front door. 'Men aren't allowed!' came a voice from behind the locked door, 'This is a women's charitable organisation and we don't want to be disturbed. Leave us alone!'

'No it's not! It's a knocking shop!' countered Kevin.

'How dare you!' replied the voice, indignantly.

Damien guessed that the voice belonged to the ugly woman they had met when they first arrived at the flat earlier that evening.

'Come-off it, love,' he said, his voice heavy with sarcasm, 'the game's up – or rather the pretence is up. We've seen one bloke come out of your flat and another go in the last half-hour. We know what you're up to.'

'Wait a minute,' replied the voice after a moment's hesitation. The woman went back up the stairs. After a few moments she came back down to the front door.

'OK, so what are you going to do about it then?'

'Put the rent up, of course,' Kevin replied without a moment's hesitation.

'Oh,' she replied with surprise and relief. She went back up the stairs again.

Damien and Kevin waited for a few minutes. Then they heard footsteps walking down the stairs back to front door.

'How much?'

'One thousand five hundred quid a month, from the beginning of next month,' said Kevin. There were frantic whispers on the other side of the door.

'And you promise not to say anything to anyone?'

'Cross our hearts and hope to die,' replied Damien and Kevin.

'Or tell the police or anything?'

'No, we only want the money,' replied Kevin, truthfully.

'The tenancy agreement says nothing about compliance with the public decency laws' added Damien, trying to sound as reasonable as possible.

'Fair enough' replied the voice, 'We've got a deal.'

'Fine,' said Kevin. 'Just deposit the dosh on the first of every month in Mr. Dunglenning's account and there'll be no problems.' Damien and Kevin could hear urgent whispers on the other side of the door. Then there was another empty pause (not a pregnant pause though, these girls knew how to look after themselves). They were just about to leave when they heard one of the girls say "how about it?" to the other. Immediately there were more giggles and the second girl replied "OK, let's ask them".

The front door opened to reveal a beautiful brunette in a black silk negligee. Her softly waving black tresses tumbled over her shoulders and caressed her magnificent breasts. She smiled at Damien and Kevin and her shapely thigh welcomed them from a split in the folds of her negligee. She licked her ruby lips with her soft, pink tongue.

'And, ummm, are you boys sure you don't want to come in for a little drink or something ……. just to close the deal….. y'know?' she asked, enticingly.

With great difficulty, they managed to take their eyes off her. They hesitated. Then, they gulped and looked at each other for a few seconds. Next, they looked back at the woman and cleared their throats nervously. Damien's strawberry jam complexion had darkened to the colour of jellied quince.

Then, as they say in the better quality Sunday newspapers, they made their excuses and left.

Or, at least, that's what they told Alaistair.

Learning from Experience

So the moral of this immoral tale is that you can never plan for retirement too early or be too careful about how you do it.

Day 2 You Know you are Old When You Understand What is Wrong with You

I was sitting in the tennis club bar the other day having a beer with some friends after a game of tennis. Jill, she's married to Martin the surgeon and has known me for a few years, was talking about novels. She asked me whether I had read any good books recently and I told her that I hadn't read any novels for over 40 years, but I had just read a very interesting book about the history of money.

Jill looked at me as if I was a Martian and asked me why I didn't read novels. I had no idea how to answer the question –

Finally, I managed to reply,

'I suppose what you're really asking me is whether I'm interested in other people' I said.

'Well, yes, but there's more to novels than that' said Jill, with a cheery smile.

' How much more?' I asked, not really caring whether she could answer my question or not.

'Well, there's the story and the narrative and how it develops and how people relate to each other as the plot thickens', she continued.

'But it's not real, though, is it? I replied. 'I mean, it's only a story'

'Yes, but it's interesting to read about how people think and how people react to situations as they develop', she persevered.

I didn't understand quite what she was saying.

'Do you learn any interesting new facts while you are reading these stories?' I asked, 'I mean, like why do banks go bust or whether the Higgs Boson particle really exists?

'Not in the stories I read', she replied, smiling sweetly, through red lipstick.

'You're not really into literature then, are you', she continued.

'It's just that I struggle with it', I replied. 'All this stuff about "he did this" and "she said that" and "Mary couldn't understand why Jane thought Ian wasn't aware that she was having an affair with Brian, when they both played tennis together?" '

'Sounds obvious to me' replied Jill.

'Well it's a complete mystery to me', I said

'It's all about empathy', explained Jill.

Well, we carried on drinking and chatting for a while about tennis and holidays and recipes and all the other things that middle class people in Lee-on-the-Solent like to talk about it, when all of a sudden, I turned to Jill.

'I've never understood why people think I lack empathy', I said

'That's because you lack empathy', came the slingshot reply.

'How do you know'? I asked.

'Because if you did have empathy, even a little bit, you'd understand why people think you didn't have any. But you don't, so you can't. See what I mean?'

I struggled with this for a moment.   .

'On the other hand, if you *did* have empathy, people wouldn't think that you didn't have it and you'd know that anyway, you wouldn't have to ask.'

'That's very insightful', I replied

'No', she replied, smiling seraphically, 'it's *empathic.*'

I nodded, as if I understood, when, really, I didn't, and took a comforting sip of beer, instead.

One of the dilemmas about lacking empathy is that it is most unlikely that you will ever find out unless somebody actually tells you. The reason for this is that people who lack empathy have no understanding of the effect their behaviour has on others because they cannot see things from anybody else's point of view. The best you can hope for with people who lack empathy is that they will believe that they are OK and that they have never done anything worse than anyone else, even if they have. Because they only see other people's behaviour and not the intentions behind they behaviour, they are not good at judging the character of other people and are absolutely useless at understanding that others might have a higher purpose in life that overrides daily concerns. Because normal people do have empathy, they find people like me to be cold and strange and are often reluctant to give us any feedback when we our conduct falls short.

Women, of course, are normally more empathic than men, which is why they tend to use indirect forms of speech so much. I finally understood, after about a million years that when your wife, girlfriend, colleague etc. asks you whether you would like to go for a walk on the beach, what she really means is:

"I want to go for a walk on the beach and I want you to come with me".

This explains why for low-empathy males like me, telling the truth is a great way to upset your wife. Thanks to the wisdom of age, of course, I now understand how this works and always lie through my teeth whenever a woman says anything to me that begins with any of the following phrases:

1. Would you like to.......?
2. Do you think that........?
3. Are you interested in....?
4. What do you think about..?

For low empathy people, it's a revelation to see how well lying really works.

These new insights came in really handy the other day when my son came to talk to me about a problem he'd been having with a girl he liked. Her name was

'Jazz' and she was really nice so I was hoping that I would be able to give him some useful advice to help him get his leg over (sorry, I mean to help him build and develop a meaningful relationship with her).

Anyway, he'd spent some time with her and eventually plucked-up the courage to ask her out. She'd declined, sadly, and said she just wanted to be friends. He hadn't been able to decode this properly and started to say that he knew that he could change her mind and make it something more than that. Tactfully (well, tactfully for me, that is), I explained that when a girl says she just wants to be friends it means she doesn't fancy you and doesn't really want to be your friend either and that there is nothing you can do about it. It took a while for this to sink in. But he's bright lad and he got the idea in the end. I know because I tested him afterwards

'What does it mean when a girl asks you whether you want to go shopping with her?', I asked.

'It means she wants you to go to the shops with her, stand around while she looks at clothes and tell her that everything looks nice on her. It doesn't mean she's actually going to buy anything and if she does it will be for her, not me'.

Bullseye! He got it.

Shortly afterwards, he found a really nice girlfriend and did form a lasting relationship and I like to think that I might have been able to help, even if it was in a small way.

I seem to have spent my whole life as if the world were a fishtank and I was standing outside looking at it. All the people I met were like fish swimming around amongst themselves and interacting with each other in ways that were completely incomprehensible to me. Efforts to engage with any of the fish in the tank were difficult due to the glass wall between us and my lack of understanding of their world. This prevented direct communications. When you are old, you begin to understand how the fish think and you learn to interpret the way they interact with each other. Finally, after all these years I can enter their world and almost be one of them. It's not hard, it just takes time to detect that what seems like random noise and emotion normally has a cause. Only now do I understand why the lovely Janice left me all those years ago. It's not enough to tell a girl you love her on only one occasion very early on in the relationship. It's a good start, but that's all it is - once you've said it, you have to keep on saying it, otherwise she'll think that your love for her has died.

 It's a no brainer, stupid!
 And it was all my fault.
 D'oh!

Day 1 Coming to Terms with Ageing

With two days to go, I decided to read-up on the science of ageing and turned to my old friends at the health and safety executive who seem to know a lot about the subject.

Apparently, successful ageing is all about coming to terms with changes in normal human capacity. These changes are inevitable. Here are some handy hints and nuggets of chirpy advice to bear in mind if you ever get depressed about the passing of the years.

Physical changes to our bodies may limit our maximum potential to perform, but in practice the requirements of most day to day activities do not demand full use of the available capacity. In other words, we can get still away with it, as long as we don't set our sights too high. So, if your ambition in life is to win the Royal Horticultural Society prize for the biggest gooseberry, you have many years ahead of you when you will have a chance. So, aim low and you won't be disappointed. Sex is still like being on a train to paradise but it's a slow train and it may be necessary to have a few stops on the way.

Other resources may be utilised to perform a task when capacity is limited. This is generally true, but it doesn't apply to all tasks of course. Sadly, most of the really fun tasks do have specialized resource requirements. You can try to carry them out using other resources but it's not nearly as much fun.

People may change the method that they use to carry out a task to make available additional capacity (this depends on the constraints of the task, of course). I find that having three consecutive days in every week when I drink no alcohol at all certainly provides additional capacity at the weekend. Another fab tip if you like a drink but find hangovers increasingly unpleasant is to start drinking earlier in the day and stop earlier. Make your nighcap a cup of tea and you will recover from your hangover while you are still asleep.

To the extent that age may result in decrements in absolute capacity, several outcomes are possible when a task requiring the utilisation of that capacity is performed:

    a.   A task which could be done in the past can no longer be performed. We've all had brewer's droop over the years but when you are old you even get brewer's droop when you are sober. A famous comedian once made an appallingly sexist joke that went something like this:

        "Why do old men need Viagra?"
        "because old women are so ugly"

        Personally, I think this is untrue as well as being unfair and unpleasant and we shouldn't blame the ladies for our own shortcomings in the bedroom.

b.   A task cannot be done as easily as before because changes in method do not compensate fully for the loss of capacity. Former levels of achievement can only be maintained with increased effort. This is clearly very true. I've tried to change a few of my methods over the years with mixed results. In general though, most things require more effort because when you've done everything a million times before the novelty has worn-off.

c.   Performance of the task may not be affected because demands are still within capacity or because change in method is fully effective. I think there is a real gem of handy advice hidden here. Basically, what they are saying is that, as you get older, stop doing things that are difficult, unpleasant or boring and choose the easy, fun things instead. So I for one have given-up trying to make the perfect Yorkshire pudding (I buy ready made from the supermarket). I have no interest in making the perfect souflé either and if they want a tasty dessert then jam roly poly and tinned custard is dead easy and brings back memories of school days.

d.   Overcompensation may occur so that performance is actually improved. In my case, this is extremely unlikely.

Measuring physical decrements in capacity will not enable predictions to be made about complex task performance. The degree of degeneration will be a poor indicator of the level of performance reached. It's more useful to consider the means by which performance is maintained rather than the level of performance on it own. I tried explaining this to my wife the other day, but wasn't convinced.

Because physical deficiencies develop at different rates between individuals and because the methods by which people compensate differ between people, we will expect to find a decrease in the range of activities that any one person can perform as he or she ages and an increase in the variability across people in older age groups. Even worse, different organs and processes involved in the production of behaviour age at different rates in a single person, it is impossible to assign a particular 'biological age' to any one person. Rather, we can either assess the age of each organ or process or of some level of functional performance of a well-designed task. I can define a few tasks easily enough but I'm reluctant to define my age on them!

Social factors will influence what people are prepared to do in comparison with what they are capable of doing. This is easily observed at tennis club New Year's Eve parties where old people try to dance to all the hits from 'Top of the Pops, 1973. It's not pleasant.

Family responsibilities will motivate behaviour of men in their 30s and 40s. The desire to maintain status will motivate behaviour in the decade or so after. We will expect to find disruptions in the performance of older people in maintaining their position in relation to failing performance and in younger people whose responsibilities exceed their capacity.

Improved anticipatory responses can be useful as you get older. Older people should have developed a larger repertoire of behaviours and skills that will enable them to anticipate future events and start to act before the event arrives – it's always useful to find out where the toilets are on arrival at the Mall rather than wait for the inevitable. Anticipatory control will help to compensate for loss of capacity, therefore older people would be expected to actively seek out predictable environments. In other words, old people are boring.

Possible adverse consequences of increased repertoire of response patterns:

a. Difficulties choosing a particular response leading to hesitation, indecision and disorganization.

b. Particular response patterns become generalised with age, leading to a loss of response versatility within an individual but greater variability between individuals in the same age group

c. Over time, learning what not to do in particular situations becomes as important as learning what to do. This is related to the ascription of values to particular responses – knowing what is and what is not *worth* doing. With age, the number of things that can be done in a particular situation will increase but the number of things likely to be done will decrease. This explains a lot, in my view and is partly because old people have an increased need for recovery after work, play and almost anything that's worth doing because it's fun.

The effects of age on behaviour may therefore manifest themselves as increasing stereotypical responses to a wide variety of situations as particular response patterns generalise to an increasingly diverse set of situations and as competing response modes are eliminated via negative reinforcement. Learning from past experience is not always a good thing (it can result in an unnecessarily restrictive response repertoire). We cannot therefore consider a person as 'young' or 'old' in absolute terms but only as young or old in relation to the task.

Day 0 Happy birthday to me

I had a nice surprise today. My wife treated me to a trip to the movies. When you reach 60 years of age, you get a discount on your ticket. Same with the ferry on the way over to the cinema. Afterwards, it did occur to me that neither the attendant at the ferry or the lady at the cinema had asked to see any identification when my wife asked for the discount.

That's because, until today, I didn't realise I was old.

Tips for Successful Aging

1. Start drinking earlier and stop at least 12 hours before you normally wake up so you can have your hangover and recover from it while you are asleep
2. No matter how well you think you are getting along, no matter how lovely they are, even if they tilt their heads to one side when they smile at you, always remember that young women do not fancy you.
3. Never miss an opportunity to use the toilet when travelling
4. Never trust what feels like a fart on the way – be kind to yourself, go to the loo. Never feel embarrassed about using the disabled toilets even if you are not disabled. Because you are old, nobody will challenge you because they naturally think that all old people are disabled by age anyway.
5. Erections are like public transport – you know there'll be another one along soon, but you have no idea when. So never waste an erection.
6. Only give advice to young people if they ask for it and never compare life now to how it was when you were their age. They are not interested, will not be envious or impressed. However, if asked, give useful tips such as, 'Never throw odd socks away. The minute you do, the other one will suddenly appear, as if by magic'.

Afterthoughts

Well, here I am then, 60 years old, getting used to being 60 years old and forgetting to ask for my old person's discount when I go to the cinema, as might have been expected.

I was sitting in the lounge the other Saturday afternoon having just completed a few non-essential jobs around the house. These were the kind of jobs that are rarely noticed and are even less likely to be appreciated by anyone else, even if they are noticed. Then, my wife walked into the room and looked at me.

The conversation went something like this.

Mrs Bob: "So, what are you going to do this afternoon before you go and play tennis, that's what I'd like to know?"

Mr Bob: "Errrrrr"

Mrs.Bob: "We can't have you lazing around all weekend. Don't you think you should find something to do?"

Mr Bob: "Umm, I'm practicing for retirement…."

Mrs Bob: "And I suppose you're going to spend all your time lazing around and doing nothing when you retire?"

Mr Bob: "Ah, well, I'm going to buy a retirement property in Spain so we can retire in a warm and sunny place"

Mrs Bob: "Buy me my retirement property in Spain now. I know, I'm going to make you a list of daily, weekly and monthly jobs to do around the house."

Getting the Hang of It

I was attending a business meeting in Panama City, Florida a while back. After a hard day, four of us decided to go for dinner at a nearby restaurant. I freshened-up and, not wanting to look too formal, wore a casual shirt underneath my jacket and no tie. So, we strolled along the main road and came across a place called 'The Crab Shack'. We walked in and a pretty waitress in shorts and a very small vest smiled and welcomed us.

'Taybull fer forrr?' she asked me, with a Southern drawl and smiling sweetly.

'Yes please, Miss, a table for four', I replied (I think she assumed I was the boss just because I was the oldest).

'Saay thet agin', she said with a cheeky smile

'Errr, do you mean 'Yes please Miss', or 'Table for Four'? I replied.

'Arther'll do, I lurve yer akseynt', she said, leading us to our table.

'And I love your tattoo', I said politely, while gazing innocently at her behind.

She turned to look at me, blushing and giggling and we both laughed.

It was at this point that I realized that even though most of her gorgeous body was visible and even though there was no tattoo to be seen, there was absolutely no chance that I would ever, under any conceivable circumstances, see, let alone gain access to that part of her lovely body that she had decorated with a tattoo, and somehow managed to hide under her very skimpy clothing.

And you know, now I know that I am old, I'm quite happy about that.

Printed in Great Britain
by Amazon